WRITERS ON FILE

Associate Editor: Malcolm Page

WESKER
on File

Compiled by Glenda Leeming

Methuen. London and New York

First published in 1985 in
simultaneous hardback and paperback editions
by Methuen London Ltd,
11 New Fetter Lane, London EC4P 4EE
and Methuen Inc, 733 Third Avenue,
New York, NY 10017

Copyright in the compilation
© 1985 by Glenda Leeming
Copyright in the series format
© 1985 by Methuen London Ltd
Copyright in editorial presentation
© 1985 by Simon Trussler

Typeset in IBM 9pt Press Roman
by 🅰 Tek-Art, Croydon, Surrey
Printed in Great Britain by Hazell Watson & Viney Ltd
Member of the BPCC Group
Aylesbury, Bucks

British Library Cataloguing in Publication Data

Leeming, Glenda
    Wester on file.—(Writers on file)
    1. Wesker, Arnold—Criticism and interpretation
    I. Title   II. Series
    822'.914   PR6073.E75Z/

    ISBN 0-413-58630-8
    ISBN 0-413-53660-2 Pbk

Contents

The theatre is, by its nature, an ephemeral art: yet it is a daunting task to track down the newspaper reviews, or contemporary statements from the writer or his director, which are often all that remain to help us recreate some sense of what a particular production was like. This series is therefore intended to make readily available a selection of the comments that the critics made about the plays of leading modern dramatists at the time of their production — and to trace, too, the course of each writer's own views about his work and his world.

Many of these comments, together with factual information about first performances, major revivals, and publication details, are assembled in Section 2, on the plays themselves, which are arranged chronologically in order of their composition. Section 4, 'The Writer on His Work', brings together other comments from the playwright himself, dealing with more general matters of construction, opinion, or artistic development (the items here being arranged either chronologically or thematically, as suits the author and the material).

In addition to providing a uniquely convenient source of *documentation*, the 'Writers on File' series also assembles the *information* necessary for each reader to pursue further his interest in a particular writer or work. Thus, Section 1, 'A Brief Chronology', provides a quick, conspective overview of each playwright's life and career, while Section 3 offers concise guidance to the writer's own work in non-dramatic forms, and Section 5 provides a bibliographical guide to other primary and secondary sources of further reading.

Full details will be found in these latter sections of any sources otherwise cited under short-titles; but it should be noted that only collected editions of plays are included in the 'Select Bibliography', since publication details of individual titles are included with the other factual data on each play. A short synopsis of each play immediately follows this information, and for quick reference this is set in slightly larger, italic type.

The 'Writers on File' series hopes by striking this kind of balance between information and a wide range of opinion to offer 'companions' to the study of major playwrights in the international repertoire — not in that dangerously predigested fashion which can too readily quench the desire to read the plays themselves, nor so prescriptively as to allow any one line of approach to predominate.

While we have tried to arrive at a format for the series which will enable users of one volume to find their way easily around any other, we recognize that some writers are, for example, far readier than others to talk about their own work. Others may, simply, be so prolific that it is not possible to present as full a range of critical opinion for each of their plays. And, of course — for reasons which do not necessarily have anything to do with intrinsic merits — some writers just attract a great deal more critical attention than others. For all these kinds of reasons, the compilers have been given the freedom to allow the particular qualities of their subjects, and of the critical response attracted, to dictate the precise presentation of the 'sampling' they have provided.

In the case of Arnold Wesker's plays, the compiler has rightly resisted the temptation to reflect the disproportionate critical attention (and the disproportionate praise) given to Wesker's earlier career, at the expense of later work which has often been no less distinctive, albeit less fashionably so. The initial success of the 'Wesker Trilogy', *The Kitchen*, and *Chips with Everything* is given its due here, but so too is the sheer variety of forms and tone by which Wesker has confused his critics since *The Friends*.

Often, we note how the theatre abroad has been responsible for keeping faith with Wesker at times when his work has been neglected in Britain — while at other times regional British theatres have premiered plays which, for all the expressions of critical confidence in their transferring to London, somehow never do. The fate of the aborted production of *The Journalists* planned by the RSC, and of the actual production of *The Merchant* which reached Broadway minus Zero Mostel, suggest that bad luck as well as bad managerial decision-making has played its own part in Wesker's career.

No wonder, then, that the extracts included in the 'Writer on His Work' section reflect Wesker's acute unhappiness with the conditions under which he (and most writers) so often have to work in the theatre, as well as providing some fascinating insights into his approach to his craft, and a few tantalizing examples of his sniping-back at the critics, which may be more fully traced in the Bibliography. Our theatre is the poorer for its apparent inability to accommodate the sometimes ingenuous but utterly distinctive voice of Arnold Wesker.

Simon Trussler

1932 May, born in Stepney, East London, son of Joseph Wesker, a Russian Jewish immigrant garment worker, and his wife Leah (born Perlmutter), of Hungarian Jewish immigrant family. Early childhood spent in 'Fashion Street and Flower and Dean Street, where my grandmother and my aunts lived'.

1939 Evacuated early in the war to 'five different places' in England and Wales, but from 1943 attended Upton House Technical School in Hackney, East London. Belonged briefly to Young Communist League, then to Zionist Youth Movement. 'Histrionic tendencies' led him to join an amateur acting group.

1948 Accepted by Royal Academy of Dramatic Art but failed to gain a grant, so worked at a number of jobs such as furniture-making, bookseller's assistant, plumber's mate.

1950 Called up for his two years' National Service in the Royal Air Force. Wrote long descriptive letters every day of first eight weeks; these he collected and rewrote into a 'very bad novel' which later supplied material for *Chips with Everything.*

1952 Various jobs in Norfolk — seed-sorter, farm labourer, kitchen porter — where he met his wife Dusty (Doreen) Bicker, then a waitress.

1954 Returned to London and became a trained pastry-cook.

1956 Worked in Paris for nine months as a pastry-cook, saving money to enter the London School of Film Technique. He 'would have gone on into the film industry but for two things' — first the *Observer* play competition, for which he wrote *The Kitchen,* and secondly John Osborne's play *Look Back in Anger,* in which he 'just recognized that things *could* be done in the theatre, and immediately went home and wrote *Chicken Soup*'.

1957 Met by chance Lindsay Anderson, film and theatre director, and asked him to read his short story *Pools,* as a possible subject for a film. 'Eventually that became too expensive to do', but Anderson also read *Chicken Soup with Barley* and *The Kitchen* and sent

7

them to George Devine at Royal Court Theatre.

1958   First production of *Chicken Soup with Barley*, at the Belgrade Theatre, Coventry, directed by John Dexter, transferred to London to the Royal Court for a second week. Awarded Arts Council grant of £300, which he used to marry Dusty Bicker.

1959   *Roots* commissioned by Royal Court, but 'George Devine was unhappy about it', so again the first production was at the Belgrade Theatre, Coventry, directed by Dexter, successfully transferring to the Royal Court, and briefly to the West End. Won *Evening Standard*'s Most Promising Playwright Award. His son Lindsay Joe born. Sunday-night production without decor *The Kitchen* (shorter version) at the Royal Court.

1960   *Chicken Soup with Barley, Roots*, and *I'm Talking about Jerusalem* produced as *The Wesker Trilogy* at the Royal Court, *Jerusalem* having opened earlier at the Belgrade Theatre, Coventry.

1961   *Roots* was Wesker's first play produced in the USA, in an off-Broadway production which received mixed notices. *The Kitchen* in its extended version opened at the Belgrade Theatre, Coventry, and transferred to the Royal Court. Film version of *The Kitchen* released. Having 'incited civil disobedience' against use of nuclear weapons, sentenced, along with other writers, to one month in prison. Accepted directorship of Centre Fortytwo, a cultural movement he had helped to evolve, intended to make the arts more widely accessible through trade-union support and involvement. His daughter Tanya Jo born.

1962   *Chips with Everything* opened at the Royal Court, and voted Best Play of 1962 after successful West End transfer. There were also simultaneous productions in the provinces, which opened in Sheffield and Glasgow a few days after the London premiere. Announced he was temporarily giving up writing plays to devote his energy to Centre Fortytwo, though for one of the Centre's festivals he wrote the libretto for a documentary, *The Nottingham Captain*. His son Daniel born.

1963   Television play *Menace* (written 1961) broadcast, but not generally liked. *Chips with Everything* opened on Broadway to good notices.

1964   Early version of *Their Very Own and Golden City* produced at Belgian National Theatre, and awarded Italian Premio Marzotto prize of £3,000.

1965   Off-Broadway production of *The Kitchen* had six-month run to good notices. *The Four Seasons* opened at the Belgrade Theatre, Coventry, but only with difficulty moved into the West End, to generally bad notices and an early closure.

1966   *Their Very Own and Golden City* in its revised version opened at the Royal Court Theatre to a lukewarm reception.

1967   Off-Broadway production of *The Four Seasons* badly received.

1970   After directing his own *The Friends* at Centre Fortytwo's home, the Roundhouse, Wesker resigned from the Roundhouse Trust, and on 20 Dec. persuaded the Council for Centre Fortytwo to pass a resolution dissolving itself.

1971   Wesker spent two months at the offices of *The Sunday Times* amassing background for his play *The Journalists,* but his prose account, *Journey into Journalism,* was resented by some journalists as a breach of confidence, and Wesker withheld it for some years.

1972   *The Old Ones* scheduled to open at the National Theatre, but withdrawn by Kenneth Tynan. Protests led to a new date being offered, but director John Dexter took the play to the Royal Court. *The Journalists* scheduled for production by the Royal Shakespeare Company, but rejected by majority of cast who had 'right to refuse' contracts. Wesker sued the company for breach of contract, not achieving a settlement until 1980.

1974   *The Wedding Feast* first produced at the Stadsteatern, Stockholm. *The Old Ones* well-received in workshop production in New York.

1976   Sales of the Penguin edition of the *Trilogy* (1964) reached quarter of a million. *Love Letters on Blue Paper* (originally a short story), transmitted as television play, and a stage version commissioned by National Theatre. Premiere of *The Merchant* at Stockholm Royal Dramaten.

1977   British premiere of *The Wedding Feast* at Leeds Playhouse, amateur premiere of *The Journalists* at the Criterion Theatre, Coventry, and premiere of stage version of *Love Letters on Blue Paper* at Syracuse (USA). *The Merchant,* directed by Dexter, previewed in Philadelphia (USA), where its leading actor Zero Mostel died suddenly. Production went on to open in New York, but was not successful.

9

1978   British premiere of *The Merchant* at Birmingham Repertory Theatre well received, but did not transfer to London. *Love Letters on Blue Paper* opened at the National Theatre's Cottesloe auditorium, directed by the author.

1979   Workshop production of *The Journalists* directed by Laura Sucker in Los Angeles (USA). A production of *Chicken Soup with Barley* won a gold medal for the best foreign play in Madrid. Wesker received £5000 from the National Film Development Fund to write a film script of the *Trilogy*.

1980   Commissioned by the touring theatres of Norway, Sweden, and Denmark to write a new play, which became *Caritas*; but as the subject was a fourteenth-century English anchoress, the Scandinavian theatres found it too obscure for touring purposes. Wesker sent out his play *One More Ride on the Merry-Go-Round,* an 'uncharacteristic' bawdy comedy, under a pseudonym, receiving a variety of responses. Wrote original film script *Lady Othello* and television play *Whitsun,* a version of his short story *The Visit.*

1981   *Caritas* opened at the National Theatre's Cottesloe auditorium. Professional premiere of *The Journalists* at the Wilhelmshaven Municipal Theatre, Germany.

1982   *Mothers,* four portraits on the theme of 'the mother', commissioned by Koichi Kimura for festival of one-act plays in Tokyo.

1983   *Annie Wobbler,* three female monologues, first performed by Suddeutscher Rundfunk, Germany, and directed by the author at Birmingham Repertory Studio Theatre, transferring to New End Theatre, London. Wrote *Cinders,* two-act play adapted from the book *An English Madam* by Paul Bailey, which the agents for the original material refused him permission to stage.

1984   Sept., dramatized reading of his early story 'Sugar Beet' (1953) given as part of an 'Arnold Wesker Week' on BBC Radio Norfolk. 6 Oct., *Yardsale,* a 30-minute radio play written for the actress Sheila Stefael, broadcast on BBC Radio. *Bluey,* a 90-minute radio play, commissioned by BBC for the European Radio Commission. Prepared scripts for four 90-minute TV films based on Arthur Koestler's novel *Thieves in the Night,* about Palestine under British mandate, for Norddeutscher Rundfunk. 13 Nov., *Annie Wobbler* brought to Fortune Theatre, London.

The Kitchen

Play in two parts, with an Interlude.
Written: 1956.

First production (original shorter version): Royal Court
Th., Sunday night 'production without decor', 13
Dec. and 20 Dec. 1959; (final version): Belgrade Th.,
Coventry, 19 June 1961; trans. to Royal Court Th.,
27 June 1961 (dir. John Dexter; des. Jocelyn
Herbert; with Robert Stephens as Peter and Mary
Peach as Monique).

First New York production: New Th. Workshop, 9 May
1966, trans. to New 81st Street Th., 13 June 1966.

Film version: made by unit of ACTT (film technicians
union), released 1961 (dir. Jimmy Hill).

Published: in *New English Dramatists,* 2 (Penguin,
1960); *Penguin Plays,* 2 (Penguin, 1964); (*revised
version*) London: Cape; New York: Random House,
1961; and in *Wesker,* 2.

*It begins, like all Mr. Wesker's plays, with a plain slice of
life: the cooks, cleaners and waitresses assembling for
their day's stint in the kitchen of a huge restaurant.
They talk disconnectedly, flirt, complain about their
job, their love life, their aches and pains. There are tensions between them, animosities and odd, speechless
friendships. At the centre is Peter – beautifully played
by Robert Stephens – a generous, violent, disorganized,
rather stupid German, who is having a disastrous affair
with a married waitress. The scene, which ends in the
lunch-hour pandemonium, has all the funny, warm
realism that is Mr. Wesker's peculiar gift. In the second
part, the men are lying around exhausted. They begin
fragmentarily to spin fantasies about what they would
do if the kitchen were wiped out. Only the German
shies away from his dream, inarticulately. And very
delicately Mr. Wesker begins to imply that the kitchen is
not just a place to work, it is the whole condition of life,
society, fate, what you will. The meanings are all there
but Mr. Wesker, mercifully, does not push them too
hard. In the last scene, the evening chaos is on. There is a*

row and the German, needled beyond speechlessness and all restraint, goes berserk with a chopper. The great kitchen is brought to a stop and its owner is left shouting after the German 'What is there more? What is there more?' As drama it is faultless, though I am not sure that final cry solves all the earlier issues. But at least Mr. Wesker is here posing his questions in such a way as to make you believe that he is beginning to know what his own answers are.

A. Alvarez, *New Statesman,* 11 Sept. 1959

The play's effortless authenticity is brilliantly brought to life by John Dexter's production. . . . The piece is splendidly visual: the white-hatted polyglot cooks dart about between the stoves and tables; we are made aware of the heat, the exasperation, the stealing, the flirtations between cooks and waitresses. . . . Not a scrap of food is actually used on the stage. Yet so completely persuasive are both dramatist and producer that we can almost smell the stench.

Robert Muller, *Daily Mail,* 28 June 1961

The Kitchen achieves something that few playwrights have ever attempted; it dramatizes work, the daily collision of man with economic necessity, the repetitive toil that consumes that large portion of human life which is not devoted to living. The vast roaring stoves that dominate the people who operate them: Cypriots, Cockneys, Germans, Italians, Frenchmen, Jamaicans and Irishmen, they are forced into uneasy fellowship by the fact of common employment. . . . John Dexter's direction is flawless, rising at the end of the first half to a climactic lunch-hour frenzy that is the fullest theatrical expression I have ever seen of the laws of supply and demand.

Kenneth Tynan, *The Observer,* 2 July 1961

The Kitchen to a great extent is based on a kitchen I worked in, in Paris, where the kitchen was shaped like that, and we really did cope with that many dinners a day, and there was that kind of speed. . . . But you get used to it, you get into the rhythm, and *The Kitchen* is based on that rhythm. What didn't happen, of course, is that no one broke any gas-leads. There was such a character as Peter, and other characters were drawn from the other kitchens I worked in.

Wesker, in *Theatre at Work,* p.90

The Film

I seem to have been about the only innocent at the press show who hadn't seen the play anyway and so I could look straight at it as a film, and a very cinematic-looking treatment it looked to me. In fact it was the objects, the kitchen paraphernalia and the physical action (fish-slicing, onion-chopping, egg-beating, steam, rattle, the slither of greasy plates, the varied movements of things cooking at a ferocious rate, every kind of saucepan and frying pan, the overpowering sense of heat and panic speed: all intensely filmish experiences − you don't, after all, get those eloquent close-ups of splitting sausages in the theatre) that struck just the right note of claustrophobia, hysteria, comradeliness.

The Spectator, 21 July 1961

I insisted on a strict following of the play, and we were all deluded into thinking that because its action was fragmentary it was obvious film material. But we realized that *The Kitchen* is intrinsically a theatrical concept, and to have made a film of it really required complete rethinking. That's one reason why I think that it failed.

Wesker, in *Theatre at Work,* p.89

Chicken Soup with Barley

Play in three acts, first of the 'Wesker Trilogy'.
Written: 1957.
First production: Belgrade Th., Coventry, 7 July 1958, trans. to
    Royal Court Th., 14 July 1958 (dir. John Dexter; des. Jocelyn
    Herbert; with Frank Finlay as Harry Kahn and Charmian Eyre
    as Sarah Kahn).
Revived: in repertoire with the other parts of the 'Wesker Trilogy',
    Royal Court Th., 7 June 1960 (with mainly the same credits);
    again as part of the 'Wesker Trilogy', Shaw Th., 3 Apr. 1978
    (dir. Anthony Cornish).
Published: *New English Dramatists*, 1 (Penguin, 1959); in *The
    Wesker Trilogy* (London: Cape, 1960; New York: Random
    House, 1961); and in *Wesker*, 1.

The central character is a passionate woman, Sarah Kahn (admirably played by Charmian Eyre), who has three of the Jewish characteristics in excess – love of family, generosity, and idealism – and the play charts three stages in her life. Act I, 1936. All her young friends are romantic communists. The Spanish war is at its height. It is the decade of hope. A successful anti-Mosley demonstration is in progress. Sarah can afford to be optimistic about the future and even about her shiftless husband. Roll on ten years. The war has just ended. Her daughter has married an ex-hero of the Party who has given up politics. Her husband is in and out of jobs, but mostly out, and her passion is centred on her adolescent son, who aims to be a socialist novelist. Turn ten years on again. Her husband is a permanent invalid. Her comrades are all scattered and Hungary has completed the disillusionment of her son. She sees him going the way of her husband. Old, tired, disappointed, she still has the fire in her belly. It is the fire not of an ideologue, but of a fighter. 'If you don't fight, you die.' But Mr. Wesker doesn't idealize or romanticize. He presents his heroine as a living person, nagging and tiresome and tactless as well, and the play, in spite of a little sag in the last act, is painful, true and alive. The company masters its difficulties very well.

T.C. Worsley, *New Statesman,* 15 July 1958

Mr. Wesker confronts us, as sanely as the theatre has ever done, with a fundamental issue: is there a viable middle course between welfare socialism and communism? He has written a fair, accurate, and intensely exciting play, which John Dexter has directed with a marvellous eye for its human values. Charmian Eyre, as Momma, is rather too blatantly prole, commenting on the character rather than embodying it; but I can imagine no improvement on the performances of Cherry Morris, Anthony Valentine, and Alfred Lynch.

Frank Finlay, who plays poor, dismembered Poppa, enters another category. Slumped, grinning, in his chair, Mr. Finlay mumbles his heart out so movingly that we are unable to distinguish between the petrifying of his body and the graying of his soul. This is a great performance. And Mr. Wesker, if he can survive the autobiographical stage, is potentially a very important playwright.

Kenneth Tynan, *The Observer,* 20 July 1958

If ever there was a play to muzzle the cynic it is this extraordinary document of the 1950s, now receiving a long overdue revival in the Dolphin Company's full production of Arnold Wesker's *Trilogy.*

Chicken Soup with Barley is a textbook example of the first play [*sic*] that young writers are supposed to 'get out of their system' before producing something worth while. Spanning twenty quarrelsome years, it shows Wesker obsessively squaring accounts with the family, linking domestic experience with the state of the nation, introducing a tormented would-be artist hero, and sending the audience away with a message in their hearts. The effect ought to be unspeakable. As it happens in Anthony Cornish's production, it is precisely the moving and illuminating work of every apprentice playwright's dreams.

Irving Wardle, *The Times,* 4 April. 1978

Sarah's folly both enriches and damages the play. The damage comes when Mr. Wesker, pulling himself together and remembering where he is, seems — as in Sarah's ringing curtain line, 'If you don't care, you'll die' — to put his full weight behind her.

The enrichment is more pervasive, and it fills the play with ambiguities. . . . She emerges as a particularly fascinating type of the woman who loves humanity at the expense of those near her. Not that she neglects her family: her charity does not only begin at home, it is rooted there. It is very practical; at almost every moment of the play food is being cooked or eaten or a kettle brewed. But it is a charity fatally divorced from tolerance.

Robert Cushman, *The Observer,* 9 Apr. 1978

When I saw [*Look Back in Anger*] , I just recognized that things *could* be done in the theatre, and immediately went home and wrote *Chicken Soup.* . . . When I finished *Chicken Soup* I just *felt* I'd written a worthwhile play, and asked [Lindsay Anderson] whether he'd read that . . . then Lindsay wrote me this marvellous letter in which he said, yes, you really are a playwright, aren't you? And he asked my permission to try and persuade the Court to let him direct it. That's how it began. The Court didn't put it on, because they were uncertain about it, and instead gave it to the Belgrade, to do for a week in Coventry and a week at the Royal Court.

Wesker, in *Theatre at Work,* p.81

15

Chicken Soup with Barley, about the disintegration of a politically-conscious family, could have been written about the last days of that family; but no, I had to begin at the beginning, when the son was only a child of four, and take the play through twenty years. . . . And so you see this obsession with digging back as far as possible to beginnings, in order to explain the present. And all the time I'm worried in case a clue has been missed.

> Wesker, in *Fears of Fragmentation,* p.113

Sarah has never quite been played as I intended her, being based on my mother, who was not a nagging shrew. Apparently serious things were said by her with humour. Certain militant things were said by her softly. 'You can't have brotherhood without love' — she would say something like that with a smile, she'd throw it away. . . . But Frank Finlay responded to the text. . . . Particularly in one scene, where Harry screams at Ronnie, it came from such an area of truth that it sounded like my father, and in the performance at the Royal Court it so distressed my sister that she had to flee.

> Wesker, in an unpublished interview with Glenda Leeming, quoted in *Wesker the Playwright*

Roots

Play in three acts, second of the 'Wesker Trilogy'.
Written: 1958.
First production: Belgrade Th., Coventry, 25 May 1959,
    trans. to Royal Court Th., 30 June 1959, and to Duke of
    York's Th., 30 July 1959 (dir. John Dexter; des. Jocelyn
    Herbert; with Joan Plowright as Beatie Bryant).
First New York production: Mayfair Th., 6 Mar. 1961.
Revived: in repertoire with the other parts of the 'Wesker
    Trilogy', Royal Court Th., 28 June 1960 (with mainly the
    same credits); again as part of the 'Wesker Trilogy', Shaw Th.,
    8 May 1978 (dir. Anthony Cornish).
Published: Penguin, 1959; in *The Wesker Trilogy* (London:
    Cape, 1960; New York: Random House, 1961); and in
    Wesker, 1.

Any bare account . . . is in danger of making it seem just the kind of play people tend to shy off. 'Oh, no, that sounds too depressing', they say, hearing that it is about a family of boorish, graceless, taciturn Norfolk farm labourers realistically and faithfully observed.

But go to the Duke of York's and you will not be depressed. You will be elated by the performance of Miss Joan Plowright; you will be held by Mr. John Dexter's production; you will be delighted by the fine naturalistic acting of the cast from Coventry's Belgrade Theatre; and you will find in the author, Mr. Arnold Wesker, a new playwright who knows how to write dialogue and to build up his tensions and climaxes, and who observes his characters with a humorous and tender affection.

Miss Joan Plowright plays the daughter, Beatie, who has gone off to London and picked up with a young intellectual. In these years, she has learned a lot of his jargon, and, returning to her benighted family, tries to pass on something of what she has learned from him. What is so admirable about Mr. Wesker's handling of his theme is that he sees all round the problem. Beatie in London has learned more than just the jargon from her Ronnie: she dimly sees that life need not be so nasty and brutish as her family made it. . . . But having never learned to express herself, all she can do is quote Ronnie at them and you can imagine the bored indifference (turning to exasperation) on those solid, silent Norfolk faces as Ronnie's views on art and living are flung in front of them day after day, in her garbled, half-hysterical version.

But Beatie fights through it, through the indifference and the inattention and one very severe reverse, and her triumph at the end (and it is Miss Plowright's triumph too) is to find at long last that her own voice comes through. She can drop quoting Ronnie and find words to express herself.

The acting and directing deserve more space than I can give them. John Dexter, the director, has been extremely daring in his use of slowness and silence. Accustomed to slickness and speed, we may find it difficult to accept his pace at first; but he insists from the start and soon takes us with him. Ponderous slowness, pointless reiteration, stubborn taciturnity, cowlike vacuity – I have never seen these so perfectly caught on the stage. But the fact that they manage to be neither boring nor depressing is the highest tribute I can pay to Mr. Dexter and his admirable cast.

T.C. Worsley, *Financial Times*, 31 July 1959

17

This cruelly efficient study of farm workers in Norfolk was an amalgamation of the pinpoint realism of the Moscow Art Theatre and Britain's kitchen-sink school of painting. Indeed, so much of the action centred upon the cracked enamel sinks of the Beales and the Bryants that water, in bucket, washing-up bowl, and tin bath, provided a constant splash of background music.

The candid realism was conveyed throughout by Wesker's dialogue, sometimes crude but always genuine, by Jocelyn Herbert's scruffy cottage settings, and by John Dexter's direction, which had the cast champing their way through fried bread for minutes on end without a murmur.

Peter Jackson, Plays and Players, July 1959

I have now seen this great, shining play three times, and it seems to have grown visibly in stature each time. It is the central pillar of Mr. Arnold Wesker's mighty Trilogy, and it is the one on which the whole arch depends. . . . The simple story still grips the audience as it grips the boards. Beatie Bryant is still the un-awakened flower, quoting her townee lover to her inarticulate, uncomprehending country family, and not really understanding his talk herself. . . . Her betrayal by her Ronnie is still poignant beyond the reach of anything but the very greatest poetry, and her final triumphant budding is still the most heart-lifting single moment I have ever seen upon a stage.

Bernard Levin, Daily Express, 20 June 1959

The second production in this overdue revival of Arnold Wesker's Trilogy again reawakens the admiration of twenty years ago and leaves you wondering how Wesker, even at that time, had acquired the reputation of a preacher. . . . Beatie Bryant goes back to her Norfolk family and bends their ears with Ronnieisms for three acts until he jilts her in the name of the higher truth. By then, your antipathies are fairly evenly divided against the bovine family, Beatie's bossy parrot cries, and the intellectual prig in the background. Then, in the miraculous final speech, Beatie begins to think for herself, and Wesker triumphantly gets his point across.

The part gave Joan Plowright a great personal success in the 1950s: but I suspect that Frances Viner's performance, often extremely irritating and as mean as the surrounding family, is closer to Wesker's idea of the character. With Plowright you felt that she would be all right anyway; with Miss Viner it is a moment of real transformation when she breaks out of her inherited shell.

Irving Wardle, *The Times,* 9 May 1978

George Devine was unhappy about it, and felt that I should combine the first and second acts into one act, and make the last act the second act, and write a new third act, in which Ronnie would appear. I thought this missed the whole point of the play, so it was not taken up by the Court. Then Peggy Ashcroft read it, and admired it, and felt that this was a part for Joan Plowright, who said she'd be prepared to do it, anywhere. The combination of the play and Joan Plowright wanting to do it induced the Belgrade to put it on, and then the Court brought it in. And the Trilogy followed.

Wesker, in *Theatre at Work,* p.82

Other reviews of the first production of Roots *are accessibly assembled in* Post-War British Theatre Criticism, *ed. John Elsom (Routledge, 1971).*

I'm Talking about Jerusalem

Play in three acts, third of the 'Wesker Trilogy'.
Written: 1958-59.
First production: Belgrade Th., Coventry, 4 Apr. 1960, trans., in a revised version, to Royal Court Th., in repertoire with the other parts of the 'Wesker Trilogy', 27 July 1960 (dir. John Dexter; des. Jocelyn Herbert).
Revived: again as part of the 'Wesker Trilogy', Shaw Th., 12 June 1978 (dir. Anthony Cornish).
Published: Penguin, 1960; in *The Wesker Trilogy* (London: Cape, 1960; New York: Random House, 1961); and in *Wesker,* 1.

I'm Talking about Jerusalem *covers the years 1946 to 1959. It thus runs concurrently with the latter part of* Chicken Soup *and the whole of* Roots, *ending with an epilogue in which the family come together again. . . . Sarah Kahn's daughter Ada and her husband Dave move from London to a desolate part of Norfolk where they intend to build the new Jerusalem, severing themselves*

19

from industrial society to create an ideal of harmonious unity between work, family life, and nature. The ensuing action is mobilised so as to put this experiment to the test.

To begin with, Dave supports his family by working as a labourer for a gentleman farmer: this prop is swiftly kicked from beneath him when he is dismissed for petty theft, and from then on he is alone, struggling to eke out a living as a craftsman, and constantly subjected to the destructive criticism of local people and old friends who regard his experiment as crazy. Driven to breaking point by the snide comments of his wife's two old aunts, he declares himself a prophet.

The play belongs at least as much to the wife as it does to Dave, for at every crisis it is her decision that stops him from giving up, and her earnest, didactic manner which carries the arguments with which Mr. Wesker seems most strongly to align himself. . . . The Belgrade production certainly emphasized the stiffness of the writing; many parts require a florid Jewish style which the company were unable to approach. And Mr. John Dexter's direction, alternating between extreme rapidity and exasperatingly over-sustained pauses, gave the text little chance to breathe.

The Times, 5 April 1960

Jerusalem is the most patchily acted of Mr. Cornish's productions, and yet it still makes a solider impact than its rather flimsy reputation promised. Play one ends in what you might call macropolitical disillusion, and play three, like play two, involves a micropolitical experiment. . . . But Dave Simmonds and his wife Ada *née* Kahn are obliged to abandon their exercise in country living and craftsmanship, and it ends by proving nothing except perhaps that it is foolhardy to blinker yourself to industry, technological progress, and the city. It's an honest deduction but one clearly distressing to Wesker, whose dramatic surrogate, Ronnie, openly blubs outside the deserted carpentry shop.

'We must be bloody mad to cry', he wails, a closing line that half-echoes Sarah's last words in *Chicken Soup,* 'you've got to care or you'll die'. Utopia remains as elusive and remote as ever, yet virtue consists in continuing to strive for it. That's the tacit conclusion of the trilogy, and the code by which Wesker has gone on writing, though not often, it has to be admitted, as vividly and attractively. The Shaw's revival is an apt reminder, at a time when it is fashionable to shrug him off, of the playwright he once

was, to some extent still is, and may one day be again.
Benedict Nightingale, *New Statesman,* 16 June 1978

I'm Talking about Jerusalem took shape in my mind. . . . But then, when *Roots* was acclaimed, I almost didn't write the third play, because I looked through the pages I'd already done, and felt, my God, this can't possibly be as good as the last one. And I had to leave it for three months before I had the stomach to go on.

Wesker, interviewed by Robert Muller,
Harper's Bazaar, Oct. 1960

I know that when I began Jerusalem, I wanted somehow for it to have a different feeling from the first two plays, that I wanted somehow not to have a conventional three-act play − somehow to break out. I suppose it must be considered the most flawed of the three, there's something wrong, and I think what's wrong is that there is this impulse to break out that I never quite fulfilled − until *Chips,* and in *Chips* it falls into place.

Wesker, in an unpublished interview with Glenda Leeming,
quoted in *Wesker the Playwright,* p.54-5

Chips with Everything

Play in two acts.
Written: 1960.
First production: Royal Court Th., 27 Apr. 1962, trans. to
Vaudeville Th., 12 June 1962 (dir. John Dexter; des. Jocelyn Herbert; with Frank Finlay as Corporal Hill, John Kelland as Pip, Colin Campbell as Chas, and Ronald Lacey as Smiler); almost simultaneous productions at Glasgow Citizens' Th., 31 Apr. 1962 (dir. Callum Mill) and at The Playhouse, Sheffield, 31 Apr. 1962 (dir. Geoffrey Ost).
First New York production: Plymouth Th., 1 Oct. 1963.
Published: London: Cape; New York: Random House, 1962; in *New English Dramatists,* 7 (Penguin, 1963); and in *Wesker,* 2.

Its subject is life as a Royal Air Force recruit. . . . The play covers the eight weeks of training, from the first assignment to a hut

21

to the formal passing-out. During that period one rebel has been broken and one pathetic misfit is still to be wrenched into place.

The merit of the play is in its savage documentation of Air Force drilling and discipline. The cast has had a thorough going-over by a retired regimental sergeant major, and Chips with Everything *owes as much to ex-RSM Brittain as to John Dexter, who has staged the piece in Jocelyn Herbert's craftily economical sets. . . .*

J.C. Trewin, *Birmingham Post,* 30 Apr. 1962

Sending up the Air Force may mean different things at different times – in war and in peace, for instance. . . . Some people in last night's audience . . . went on tittering at scenes of square bashing which, like most things Mr. Wesker writes, were in fact intensely earnest. . . . Not that the play has not its funny moments: the raid on a coke dump is a beautifully timed dumb-show and there is good natural reporting of the talk to be heard in any hut or NAAFI. But Mr. Wesker's airmen are the truest I have seen on any stage and make Mr. Rattigan's [in] *Ross* melodramatic and Mr. Livings's [in *Nil Carborundum*] like comic postcards compared to documentary film.

The making of conscripts into airmen is the killing of men as men. Most of them conform in a predictable way. One of them is broken and put back for another try. This is Smiler – the one who has to keep saying 'It's natural, Corporal, I was born that way', played by Ronald Lacey – but he is only the useful casualty who throws up the main study. The heart of the play is with the upper-class rebel, a cleverly chosen hero onto whom to swing the play's considerable emotional weight. This Thompson is the father-hating conscript from a posh home whose mutinous instinct is something which he himself does not fully understand. He makes his gesture of defiance, only to find that his mates are not really with him. 'They', the officers, the men of his own background 'get' him too, by showing him the weakness of his position which is his desire to 'play Messiah to the masses'. And the strength is gone out of him. . . .

Philip Hope-Wallace, *The Guardian,* 28 Apr. 1962

Arnold Wesker's new play at the Royal Court makes a dazzling evening. The play combines some of the best elements of *The Kitchen* with some of the best of *Roots.* It has the fluid, rapid

organization of the former and the social content of the latter. Structurally, it is most daring and experimental, and, as I think, completely successful. Those who have put Mr. Wesker into the category of the dreary four-walled realists must now think again. He has broken right out of the naturalism of his Trilogy and has found a form that allows him to express his feeling and ideas implicitly without any of that preaching which was the weakness of the earlier plays. And this free and fluid form has been translated by his director, Mr. John Dexter, into a production of astonishing virtuosity. . . . His play, of course, is not 'about' the RAF. It is not just a crude attack upon the way officers treat the men. It is not even 'about' the English class system, though this is nearer the point. What the play does is to bring into sharp focus the moral and spiritual damage which our class relationships do to people as people. . . . It needs great organization to keep this kind of play flowing, and Mr. Wesker achieves it. So, too, he has broken through the naturalistic speech barrier; and by using the greatest restraint and tact in the language of his totally unpretentious soliloquies, he is able to pass to and fro between them and the demotic dialogue without any uncomfortable jerks.
Financial Times, 30 Apr. 1962

What an anathema it is! In construction, superb; in writing, imaginative and touching; in symbolism, reverent and moving; in irony, corrosive and overwhelming. . . . I view with ambiguity the play's ending, in which the panoply and music of military glory are used in ironic triumph to celebrate the imminent death of two souls, one rich and educated, one stupid and poor, each the sacrificial victim of the officer class, the privileged, the rulers. As a member of the Athenaeum and MCC, I view it with misgiving; as a dramatic critic, I will cheer till I am hoarse and black in the face. This is the left-wing drama's first real breakthrough, the first anti-Establishment play of which the Establishment has cause to be afraid. If there is a better play in London I haven't seen it. This is something to be discussed and re-discussed, admired, feared.
Harold Hobson, *Sunday Times,* 29 Apr. 1962

Although it invites us to rage at the rulers and to pity the ruled, it denies us the luxury of catharsis. Its purpose is not to purge us, but to prove that the body politic needs purging. We are studying a disease; and what matters is not so much the pain it inflicts as the extent to which it is curable.

Men are not born obedient. Servility is a reflex brought about by subtle and patient conditioning; and Mr. Wesker explains how the habit is formed. To begin with, the airmen are sharply individualized: but after a sustained dose of indoctrination, they are barely distinguishable from the stereotypes of British war films and Whitehall farce. They have learned their place in the hierarchy, and may some day aspire to the ambiguous, compromised status of Corporal Hill, the NCO in charge of their hut.

This last is a character beautifully observed, and as beautifully played by Frank Finlay. By birth a prole, he has gone over to the enemy, whose orders he carries out to the letter with wry, humourless gusto. Professionally bellicose on the parade-ground, he relapses when off duty into immediate sympathy with the men he has just been bullying; and though he is unaware of the paradox, Mr. Wesker sees to it that we are not.

Kenneth Tynan, *The Observer*, 6 May 1962

Even the opening of *Chips* was designed as a blow against standard metropolitan practice. Instead of giving a London management a monopoly on the play for the duration of its run, [Wesker] offered it to eight provincial companies. . . . Only one of the eight (Glasgow) accepted: the others turned it down, principally on grounds of production costs. Undeterred by this, the Sheffield Playhouse (not one of the eight) gallantly made a bid for the play and, by casting outside the company, assembled a production which opened last Monday. . . . The result has nothing like the polish of John Dexter's production at the Court, but in some ways I suspect it is closer to the anatomy of the original. . . . What comes over is a bitterly personal expression of loathing for the class tyranny of service life; and it is this which is muffled in the naturalistic Court production.

Irving Wardle, *The Observer*, 6 May 1962

Chips was more a jumping off point. I think that the characters of Pip and Chas are two sides of myself, but this is imaginative experience rather than actual experience. . . . It has been said that the reason why [the officers] seem to be more stereotyped is because I haven't experience of them. I don't agree. I deliberately said to myself, I am not going to make them rounded characters out of any sort of liberal impulse. However rounded I might make them, they still stood for what they did. And even so, the way they spoke and the way they behaved is not caricatured, it is very real. . . . The coke-bunker scene was a deliberate attempt on my part to find a means of demonstrating a point visually, and I wrote out the detail of the whole scene. . . . *Chips* is a warning. It says — though again one is theorizing after the event — to the ruling class: you can no longer kid us. We know the way it happens. And to those who are ruled: look, boys, this is the way it happens, and this is the way it will end if you continue not to recognize that you are very sweetly but very definitely being put in your place.

Wesker, in *Theatre at Work*, p.90-2

The Nottingham Captain

'A Moral for Narrator, Voices, and Orchestra.'
Written: 1962.
First production: Wellingborough Festival, Wellingborough,
    11 Sept. 1962 (dir. Colin Graham).
Published: in *Six Sundays in January* (London: Cape, 1974).

This documentary was prepared at short notice for a Centre Fortytwo festival. Speeches by Byron, Castlereagh, and Jeremy Bentham set a scene of industrial unrest and threatening rebellion in the early nineteenth century, and the action concerns the government's employment of Oliver, an agent provocateur, to incite a pathetically ill-organized but potentially effective uprising. Three leaders, including the so-called Nottingham Captain, Jeremiah Brandreth, are hanged for treason. The material is mostly narrated, and there are alternative accompanying scores for seven-piece orchestra — one in jazz idiom by Dave Lee, and one in classical idiom by Wilfred Josephs.

Their Very Own and Golden City

'Play in Two Acts and 19 Scenes.'
Written: 1963-64.
First production: in French, National Th. of Belgium, Brussels,
    Nov. 1965 (dir. Jean-Claude Huyens).
First British production: Royal Court Th., 19 May 1966

(dir. William Gaskill, des. Christopher Morley; with Ian
McKellen as Andrew Cobham, Ann Firbank as Kate, Gillian
Martell as Jessie, and Sebastian Shaw as Jake and Maitland).
Revived: in a revised version, Municipal Th., Aarhus, Denmark,
May 1974 (dir. Wesker; des. Hayden Griffin).
Published: London: Cape 1966; in *New English Dramatists*,
10 (Penguin, 1967); and in *Wesker*, 2.

Their Very Own and Golden City *covers some sixty years, in
which a young working-class boy becomes a famous architect,
and pursues his dream of building ideal cities in England's green
and pleasant land. By the saddened end of his long life one such
city has struggled into being, but more or less strangled (and its
creator with it) by its own umbilical cord of compromise. In the
long run it is not in the least important that this tale of vision
and disillusion is clearly a projection of Mr. Wesker's work for
Centre Fortytwo. What is important is that the experience
should have been fiercely annealed in the imagination. . . . I could
wish that Christopher Morley's ingenious sets were not so
uniformly glum, and that William Gaskill's direction did not quite
so often freeze the characters to mark the end of scenes . . . thus
imparting a reverential air to proceedings already amply earnest.
But he has drawn a whole gallery of first-rate performances from
his cast.*

J.W. Lambert, *Sunday Times,* 22 May 1966

I am ambivalent about Centre Fortytwo which can be viewed as
patchwork in what is basically a society built on lunatic values,
just as the six Golden Cities are all patchwork. . . . Lindsay
Anderson read one draft, and a major criticism he made was that
he didn't know whether Cobham thought he was right to start
the Golden Cities or not. If he thought he was right, and that it
was effective, then he was a bloody fool really. And I accepted
this criticism, and thought about it, and realized that Cobham
mustn't think this. He must at some point recognize that it's
patchwork, but recognize then that there is no alternative, and
in this recognition would be reflected, it seems to me, the state
of the Left in this country. . . . Instinctively as an artist, my
inclination is not to indulge in morbidity and pessimism, and so I
flinch from the oppressive ending. And this is in direct conflict

with experience, which is so often oppressive and depressing. And the form of the flash-forward gave me the opportunity to cheat, to have two endings, in fact: the ending of the young people in the cathedral, which is still off the ground and optimistic, and the ending of the reality-stream. The problem is, whether the weight of the reality-stream isn't more depressing than the weight of the innocence-stream is encouraging.

Wesker, in *Theatre at Work,* p.92-3

After the London productions in which the director made the mistaken and crippling decision (with which I foolishly agreed) to have one set of actors play both the old and young protagonists, I thought the play was irretrievably flawed. But with the help of the Danish actors and through the brilliant set of Hayden Griffin I came to understand the play better and to discover that, though it attempts too much, it is not irretrievably flawed. . . . Because of the construction of this play — which is in the form of a 'flash forward' (as opposed to 'flash-back') — two sets of actors are needed . . . one set of young actors to whom we constantly return in the setting of the Cathedral, and another set who will act out the play from being young men and women to old ones. In the London production one set of actors played both parts and this established a particular style to the production. But in May 1974 the author directed the play in Aarhus, Denmark, where he not only reverted to two sets of actors but also made changes to the play. . . . It is in the nature of the play that the sets can begin to move into position while the previous scene is ending, thus ensuring a completely fluid style of production. . . . If the cathedral scenes in either act are heavily played this entire play will fail. Innocence, gaiety, and a touch of lunacy is their atmosphere.

Wesker, 'Preface' and 'Note' to *Wesker,* 2

The Four Seasons

Play in four parts.
Written: 1964.
First production: Belgrade Th., Coventry, 24 Aug. 1965, trans. to Golders Green Hippodrome, 9 Sept. 1965, and to Saville Th., 21 Sept. 1965.
First New York production: Theatre Four, 14 Mar. 1968.

27

Published: London: Cape, 1966; in *New English Dramatists,*
9; and in *Wesker,* 2.

*Whereas [Wesker's] previous plays have concerned themselves
with group living, this is a love story with only two characters.
A man and a woman arrive in winter at a derelict house and we
watch the development of their relationship, parallel to the
passage of the seasons. Thus it burgeons in the spring, reaches
its fullest development in a golden summer, and dies with the
onset of autumn.*

One of the characters refers to 'the drama of watching things
grow', and that is the essence of Mr. Wesker's play. . . . But,
although Mr. Wesker is constantly alert to the explosive undertow
present in any intimate relationship, perceptiveness does not of
itself constitute drama. The flaw in his play is that he totally
excludes the outside world. He does not admit that a love affair
is no less subject to economic and social pressures than anything
else.

The best moment in the evening comes when Mr. Wesker
remembers his old saw that 'the theatre is a place where one
wants to *see* things happening'. When the man proudly makes
an apple strudel to delight his love, the audience roars with
pleasure at the sight of a job visibly accomplished. Alan Bates
brings a splendid absorbed excitement to this part. Throughout
he captures the rapidly alternating moods of the character with
no sudden changes of gear: all is smooth and supple. And Diane
Cilento brings a fierce beauty and haunting sadness to her role.

The Times, 11 Sept. 1965

Of course it did occur to me that in discussing, in recreating love,
a play about love, I was not going to be touching upon social
issues, and I had to ask myself the question: 'Could I do this?
Is this valid in − not merely in theatre, but is it valid as part of a
socialist concept of art?' And I believe I decided it was, since if
you imagine the millenium, if you imagine the ideal state, you
would soon be confronted with human problems. In fact I can
make this much simpler. If I say that my attitude to socialism,
the reason why I believe as a socialist, is not because I believe
that a new economic order, when men are not competing for

survival, is going to solve problems, but because I believe there is such a problem to being a human being at all that to complicate it even more with economic problems is to confront people with the wrong battle. So this being my view of socialism it follows that once the economic battle is over there is still the battle of being alive, of being a human being. . . .

Wesker, interviewed in *Behind the Scenes*, ed.
Joseph F. McCrindle (1971)

The critics went berserk! I think for a number of reasons. Even for the most intelligent and sane critic, it still is a shock to go expecting one kind of play and to receive another. And superficially, *Four Seasons* is right out of the context of all my other plays. I think also that a play containing that kind of heightened dialogue is just too strange for ears that we have trained to accept the colloquial dialogue and ordinary rhythms of speech. So it's a question of training the critics all over again. . . . Because I wanted to recreate the feeling of a woman who hasn't the energy to do anything, I actually *have* her doing nothing. I could have had her moving around and pottering and she could have exuded lethargy and ennui and despair, and it seems to me that the critics should have understood that I simply didn't want to go through that fussy business. So the lethargy was represented by her remaining in the chair and Adam doing all the movement.

Wesker, in *Theatre at Work*, p.94-5

The Friends

Play in two acts.
Written: 1967.
First production: Lilla Teatern, Stadsteater, Stockholm, Sweden, 24 Jan. 1970 (dir. Wesker; des. Teresa Gigyksa).
First British production: Roundhouse, London, 19 May 1970 (dir. Wesker; des. Nicholas Georgiadis; with Susan Engel as Esther and Ian Holm as Manfred).
Published: London: Cape, 1970; and in *Wesker*, 3.

The friends of the title are a middle-aged group who have known each other most of their lives, the children of labouring fathers and tight-lipped mothers in the north. Down south, they have had success with a chain of shops selling wallpaper, clothes, toys, and

29

*Victorian bric-a-brac. Now they are in despair. They are bored
by the business and face bankruptcy. This dismays them less than
the knowledge that they have failed in their object, which was to
interest poor uneducated people in their wares. . . . Somewhat
unconvincingly, the play ends with a mystic rededication to life
under a giant portrait of Lenin. . . .*

The Roundhouse is a large, open arena magnificently adapted to
extrovert, drum-and-trombone play. *The Friends* is quiet chamber
music, a drawing-room play with one single, luxurious set. Last
night the actors found themselves having to speak pianissimo at
the tops of their voices. . . .

John Barber, *Daily Telegraph,* 20 May 1970

The room is enormous. It is cluttered with elegant junk. Presiding
over it is a portrait of Lenin, hanging above an enormous Victorian
bed, for the room is not just a sitting-room: it is also a sick room.

It is soon to be a death room, for the woman in bed is
dying. . . . Esther, played by Susan Engel, is as talkative on her
death-bed as the others are in their living-room. She, of them all,
is seen as the true revolutionary, spreading sweetness where the
others spread dissent.

With her death, the friends reveal the littleness of their minds,
the emptiness of their aims. But one by one they also reveal
human beings groping for love, understanding, peace, silence.
In the end, and it is an end that cliff-hangs on the edge of bathos,
they gather around the dead woman and raise her lifeless hand
in salute to the portrait. . . . This is Wesker's most ambitious
play. Though occasionally in the first act it is both sententious
and pretentious (Wesker is still talking volubly about Jerusalem)
it is bold and, finally, beautiful in its dramatic sweep as his
characters crumble before our eyes.

He himself directs this play of ideas and gets some stunning
performances from Ian Holm as the self-educating brother,
Victor Henry as the self-pitying lacerating husband, Lynn Farleigh
as a middle-class scapegoat who fights back, and John Bluthal
as a middle-aged voice of exasperated sanity. All are given
magnificent monologues by a master of this art. They rise to
the occasion.

Anthony Hern, *Evening Standard,* 20 May 1970

[In Romania] when someone dies, they lay the body on a catafalque and the mourners line up against the wall while the elders of the village dance, with phallic symbols − sticks and things − in their hands. And the dance becomes frankly erotic, even obscene. They whip themselves into a frenzy until finally they get the actual body, take it under the armpits, and dance with it. So there it is, this dead body, being danced with. It's some sort of release, the mourners laugh, and begin to dance themselves. This struck me very powerfully as a manifestation of the desperate need that men have to survive the knowledge of death; they will create extraordinary rituals for themselves so that they can live more easily with it. The image stayed with me when I was getting ready to write *The Friends*. And became the final image.

Wesker, interviewed in *Theatre Quarterly*, 28 (1977)

The New Play

Experimental play in two acts (not intended for performance).
Written: 1969.
Unpublished, but extracts appear as 'First Circle of Perception',
in a folio of screen prints based on paintings by John Allen,
Stepney Streets (London: Heritage Press, 1976); as 'Second
Circle of Perception', in a folio of etchings by Maty Grunberg,
The Second Circle of Perception (London: B. Forster, 1974);
and as 'Fourth Circle of Perception', in the programme of
The Friends, Roundhouse, 1970.

Existing only in one draft, this is an impromptu *(in the French tradition) in which Wesker presents himself in person wrestling with the problems of writing a play about old people, the play being punctuated by 'Circles of Perception', monologues uttered by the author-cum-protagonist, about his fears and beliefs.*

I was trying to write *The Old Ones*, and I had an old-fashioned blockage. And accompanying this blockage was this urge not to write plays in the old way. I was tired of the ordinary stage, with actors coming on and off and sets being changed, and with inventing slightly different characters with slightly different names. So I decided to let it all hang out, as they say. Everybody

in that play is called by their real name. There is a character
called Arnold, there is a character called Leah, who is my mother,
there are characters who are my mother's friends, there are
characters of Jennie Lee, Robert Maxwell, Harold Lever — people
who were involved in Centre Fortytwo — and my wife Dusty,
and so on. Because they all seemed to come together and form part
of my experience, which was blocking me. I was paralysed,
crippled. . . . In terms of technical structure, I used just about
everything — slides, film, the magic lantern. . . . Now I feel
it's private in a way that one shouldn't be in literature. But
I'm not sure about that. I've been very personal in so much work,
I don't know why I should baulk at that. I think there might
also be problems over libel, using people who are still alive.

Wesker, interviewed in *Theatre Quarterly,* 28 (1977), p.10-11

The Old Ones

Comedy in two acts.
Written: 1970.
First London production: Royal Court Th., 8 Aug. 1972 (dir.
John Dexter; des. Douglas Heap; with Max Wall as Manny,
George Pravda as Boomy, Patience Collier as Sarah, and Susan
Engel as Rosa).
First New York production: The Lambs, 6 Dec. 1974 (dir. Ben
Shaktman).
Published: London: Cape, 1973; *revised version:* London:
Blackie, 1974 (Student Drama Series); and in *Wesker,* 3.

The Old Ones *at the Royal Court . . . continues the quest for non-
narrative theatre begun in* The Four Seasons *and* The Friends.
*Like them it also shows Wesker moving away from the exploration
of public issues to the examination of private pain and joy. . . .
The old ones of the title are the senior members of a Jewish
family and their friends, all of whom take refuge from senility
in different ways. Emmanuel, the tailor, conquers his profound
nocturnal despair by teaching himself new physical skills; Sarah,
his sister, bakes, cooks, sews to ward off thoughts of mortality;
Boomy, his life-hating brother, indulges in competitive literary
quotation games; and Millie, Sarah's friend, retreats into her own
private world of hazy inconsequentiality. Gradually the separate*

threads and characters are drawn together as the family foregathers to celebrate the feast of Succoth; and what emerges is a traditionally Weskerian assertion of the joy of life symbolized by the family's union in a triumphal Jewish dance.

Michael Billington, *The Guardian*, 6 Aug. 1972

John [Dexter] made a physical contribution to *The Old Ones*. The original script was a simple juxtapositioning of these scenes, one alongside the other, ending in the Friday-night supper. And John said, 'I know what you're trying to do by setting up poetic juxtapositions and not having a plot or a narrative. But what it does need — no matter how delicate — is a framework within which to contain the whole piece. Is it possible to start the preparation of the Friday-night supper right from the beginning of the play?' I said, 'No, but you could prepare for a Jewish festival', and I suddenly thought of Succoth, because that had building little huts on stage and I knew John liked that sort [of thing].

Wesker, interviewed by Ronald Hayman,
The Times, 5 Aug. 1972

I suppose it's as simple as that I had an enormous admiration for my mother and her cronies, her band of extraordinary old ladies. Sarah is the still centre, surrounded by these extraordinary old people who find all sorts of ways to survive and carry on. . . . I'm full of admiration for all the relatives, aunts, and uncles, who are mixed into the play — a very extraordinary mixture of tough personalities who were good and vivid and seemed to make significant patterns. . . . You can imagine that all the old ones in all the plays are the same people.

Wesker, interviewed in *Theatre Quarterly*, 28 (1977), p.11

The Journalists

Play in two acts.
Written: 1971.
First amateur production: Criterion Th., Coventry, 27 Mar. 1977 (dir. Geoff Bennett).
First professional production: Landesbuhne, Wilhelmshaven, Germany, 10 Oct. 1981 (dir. Klaus Hoser).
Published: London: Writers and Readers Co-operative, 1975; in

The Journalists: a Triptych (London: Cape, 1979); and in
Wesker, 4

We are in the offices of The Sunday Paper *and the action
switches, in short cinematic takes between the Editor's office,
the foreign desk, features, sport, business, the women's page, the
arts page, and In Depth. Each page has its own obsessions. But
the key narrative thread is provided by an acid female political
columnist's attempt to link a left-wing MP with a group of
young angries who rob supermarkets for old-age pensioners and
do bank heists to pay strikers. And in a slightly melodramatic
conclusion, we discover the columnist's own son is one of the
young robbing hoods.*

That, however, is neither here nor there. What matters is
Wesker's ironclad conviction that our Lilliputian society is
governed by a need to cut giants down to size and that the press
is a major part of that process. . . . But though one might cavil at
Wesker's thesis, there is no denying the play's originality of form
or richness of content. I can think of no recent play about the
media that raises so many probing questions and that captures so
well that blend of light banter and heavy industry that characterizes
a newspaper office. . . . Like Wesker's earlier work play, *The
Kitchen, The Journalists* also depends on a slowly accelerating
rhythm which Geoff Bennett's production accurately captures.
Michael Billington, *The Guardian,* 25 Mar. 1977

I had a number of journalists, and I had one particular friend
who was a journalist − in fact, that same lady to whom the play
is dedicated. I wanted to make sure that I didn't perpetuate
any clichés about journalists and the atmosphere in which they
work, but I didn't want to write a play about journalism as such.
I wanted to explore what I called the Lilliputian mentality, a kind
of mentality with which I've been obsessed for a long time. . . .
It seemed to me that journalism was an area in which I could
explore this Lilliputian mentality. . . . Like most people I'm very
ambivalent about journalism. . . . The tendency seems to me to
be to diminish achievement, to concentrate on blemishes. . . .
Then other ideas crept in. To what extent does the journalist
damage himself when he engages in constant attacks on

others? ... And how often does one encounter the mean-spirited person who feels he is compelled to reduce people to his own miserable level? Journalism could be a mirror of that aspect of human behaviour.

Wesker, interviewed in *Theatre Quarterly,* 28 (1977), p.13

Love Letters on Blue Paper

Play in one long act.

Written: 1976, adapted from his short story and television play of the same title (see p.44).

First production: Syracuse Stage, Syracuse, 14 Oct. 1977 (dir. Arthur Storch).

First London production: Cottesloe Th. at the National Th., 15 Feb. 1978 (dir. Wesker; des. Bernard Culshaw; with Elizabeth Spriggs as Sonia, Michael Gough as Victor, and Kenneth Cranham as Maurice).

Published: London: TQ Publications, 1978; and in *Wesker,* 3.

A trade-union boss is dying of leukaemia. His wife, though supposedly ignorant of his fate, writes him letters celebrating their marriage. That, really, is the whole play, and there are certainly times when you wonder if it is enough. ... Some may argue that no play can survive such spectacular wartlessness at its centre. Others, including myself, would reply by pointing to the less sentimentally conceived parts of Wesker's obsequies: the nice young confidant, whose own terminal response to the imminent passing of his chum is a sudden, heartfelt 'thank God it's not me' ... above all the wife, busy with the washing and washing-up as her epistolatory ardour comes over the theatre tannoy. Michael Gough, who plays her beloved, may seem to us to smell a little too strongly of sanctimony. To her he doesn't, and it is her view that finally and rather surprisingly prevails, partly because of Elizabeth Spriggs's po-faced, mulish, and utterly unposturing playing of the part, and partly because the love-letters Wesker has concocted for her have a strange and haunting authenticity. ... Only Wesker, of our dramatists, would presume to prise the heart from its standard slot and hang it so openly on the sleeve. And only Wesker could get away with it.

Benedict Nightingale, *New Statesman,* 24 Feb. 1978

I had no idea that Vic Feather [former General Secretary of the TUC] was dying of leukaemia — that was a rather macabre coincidence. The original story was written long before I heard that news. But the *character* was certainly based on Vic Feather — hence the use of the same name. . . . The other ingredient was the personality of an old friend of mine called Robert Copping. . . . One day he came back, dying of leukaemia. I watched him for some days in Guy's Hospital, dying. And his wife Valerie showed me some letters . . . one describing how he first was told that he had leukaemia, and the other telling how, after the initial shock he began to think that 'Karl Marx is dead, Freud is dead. . . '. And somewhere in the play is my relationship with Dusty too.

Wesker, interviewed in *Theatre Quarterly,* 28 (1977), p.20

The Wedding Feast

'A play in two acts and a prologue, freely adapted from a short story called *An Unpleasant Predicament* by Fydor Dostoevsky.'
Written: 1972.
First production: Stadsteatern, Stockholm, Sweden, April 1974, (dir. Gun Arvidsson).
First British production: Leeds Playhouse, 20 Jan. 1977 (dir. John Harrison and Michael Attenborough; des. John Halle; with David Swift as Louis Litvanov).
Revived: Birmingham Repertory Th., 5 June 1980 (dir. Peter Farago; des. Christopher Morley; with David Suchet as Louis Litvanov).
Published: in *Plays and Players,* April and May 1977; and in *Wesker, 4.*

The hero, Louis Litvanov, is an immigrant shoe manufacturer who still sees himself as a peasant and sets up as a model employer; caving in to his workers' demands, throwing all-night parties for them, and driving to work in an old Ford with his Rolls reserved for weekends. His double life is put to the test when he wanders, uninvited, into the wedding party of one of his men, and is left, after a climax of drunken violence, to acknowledge that bosses cannot change sides.

The Wedding Feast is modestly described as a free adaptation of a Dostoevsky story, but it speaks throughout in Wesker's voice and shows his talent, becalmed in *The Friends* and *The Old Ones,* getting into its stride again. . . . Whether or not the play dramatizes an economic barrier, it certainly illuminates a cultural division. As the party thaws out from hideous embarrassment to exchanges of jokes, toasts, dances, and a party game that turns ugly, the two sides might as well be speaking in different languages. . . . All that is orchestrated in great detail and could produce a shimmering atmosphere of absurdity and pathos with abrupt moments of stabbing revelation. It does not achieve that effect in John Harrison's halting production, but the performances of David Swift, benevolently thick-skinned to the last, and Fiona Walker as his Marxist secretarial adversary carry a strong idea of the play's latent power.

Irving Wardle, *The Times,* 22 Jan. 1977

When Arnold Wesker's funny and disturbing play was first staged in Britain at Leeds in 1977, five years after it was written, it seemed certain that it would transfer to London and reach the wider audience it deserves. But it didn't. Now, in these leaner dramatic times, Peter Farago's deft production emphasizes that this is Wesker's best work, a brilliant and complex comedy that surely must come to London. . . . Wesker sets up his situation with an over-emphatic narrator, eager that we miss nothing. And his conclusion may be dubious, as Litvanov surveys the mess and wreckage of the morning after, still melancholy at his recollections of the results of his rash action, and decides: 'Yes, that's the way it has to be.' But the actual party is a beautifully observed, movingly funny, marvellously constructed confrontation that begins in embarrassment and ends in humiliation. . . . David Suchet's performance is a perfect blend of energy, aggressive sentimentality and genuine affection that is denied an outlet within his marriage. And there is excellent support from the remainder of the cast.

John Walker, *Now! Magazine,* 13 June 1980

Let's remember that it was originally a film script . . . here is an ironic look at the worker-employer relationship. . . . Even though the original film script was about an Italian, because Anthony Quinn was an Italian, the man was actually so Jewish that when I finally made it into a play it was inevitable that I

37

should make him Jewish, not Italian. . . . I think the first act works marvellously. . . . In retrospect, I began to wonder whether I was all wrong, when people were turning down the play because they claimed that the first act was so different from the other two . . . but it eliminated all that awful plot-making that so often prevents the process of the play from unfolding.

Wesker, interviewed in *Theatre Quarterly*, 28 (1977), p.17-18

The Merchant

Play in two acts.
Written: 1975-76.
First production: Royal Dramatenteater, Stockholm, 8 Oct. 1976 (dir. Stefan Roos).
First English-language production: Plymouth Theatre, New York, 16 Nov. 1977 (dir. John Dexter; des. Jocelyn Herbert; with Joseph Leon as Shylock, John Clements as Antonio, and Roberta Maxwell as Portia).
First British production: Birmingham Repertory Th., 12 Oct. 1978 (dir. Peter Farago; des. Christopher Morley; with David Swift as Shylock, Frank Middlemass as Antonio, and Angela Down as Portia).
Published: in *Wesker*, 4; *revised version*: London: Methuen, 1983 (Methuen Student Editions).

One is first prompted to ask: what would Shakespeare have said? The question is neither frivolous nor irrelevant. In a very real way The Merchant *is Mr. Wesker's reply to Shakespeare, his exploration of Shakespeare's antisemitism, itself fairly conventional for Elizabethan times. . . . Wesker sees Shylock and the merchant, Antonio – Jew and Christian – as close friends, indeed loving friends, who would literally do anything for each other. It is a friendship strengthened by the prevailing antisemitism of Venice, a fact of their lives which both recognize and ignore. The bond itself – that terrible pound of flesh – is nothing but a harsh joke by Shylock, to show a mocking contempt for Venetian law, a law that insists that in any transaction between Jew and Christian a written bond must exist. . . . There are lovely resonances of the original play here – such as when Bassanio coldly contemplates the caskets, trying to second-guess the whimsical madness that led a father to let his daughter be thus won. Or again when Wesker at last quotes Shakespeare direct – with the 'Has not a Jew eyes' speech, which he puts into the mouth of the play's unsympathetic character, only to have Shylock declare: 'I will not have pleas made on behalf of my humanity'. Shylock's pride is for justice – so the consideration that, in his way, he is as good as Gentile, he sees for the patronizing clap-trap it is. . . .*

The trial scene is a gem of staging, and the hurly-burly of the Venice Ghetto is poetically evoked. The acting, while at times almost dominated by the ghost of Zero Mostel, who should have played Shylock, swoops up to the occasion. . . . The play raises issues and teems with life as a consequence. It is regrettable that Broadway decided to reject The Merchant *and that it closed after a handful of performances.*

Clive Barnes, *The Times,* 3 Dec. 1977

Merchant, which opened yesterday at the Plymouth Theatre, is a play of ideas. It is provocative, generally intelligent, and sometimes strained or confused. Its writing has moments of ferocious brilliance and wit; on the other hand, its dramatic structure is weak and its dramatic impact fitful and uncertain. . . . Joseph Leon . . . plays the part with liveliness, humour, and moments of real passion. He has his triumphs; there is a heartbreaking instant when he prepares to stab Antonio in the courtroom and his hands, accustomed only to turning pages and gesticulating in arguments, literally stammer as they hold the knife. . . . Mr. Wesker's language lives, but sporadically: the evening is stimulating but only sometimes successful.

Richard Eder, *New York Times,* 17 Nov. 1977

It is a thoroughly original work, with Shakespeare's words surfacing only briefly and adroitly among the elegant speeches that are typical of Mr. Wesker. His language is not always dramatic, but there is, in *The Merchant,* a compelling play to be found – a play that works ingeniously as an ingenious theatrical puzzle, with debts to history and social structures that Shakespeare never found, and as a passionate document. . . . Peter Farago's production somewhat tones down the Hitler Youth behaviour of Bassanio and his friends, as David Swift's intelligent performance makes mellow the humour of Shylock's rabbinical spirit. It is a tract for intelligence and understanding, and also, too parenthetically, for the good to be found in freedom for women. . . . Angela Down appears humbly, as a woman, with a solution that Venice is desperate to have, and then reluctantly turns to her future as a wife.

Ned Chaillet, *The Times,* 17 Oct. 1978

It was the Jonathan Miller production of Shakespeare's *The Merchant of Venice* which I didn't like, and I certainly detested Olivier's 'oi, oi, oi,' sort of Jew. When Portia suddenly gets to the bit about having a pound of flesh but no blood, it flashed on me that the kind of Jew I know would stand up and say, 'Thank god!' My first thought was that perhaps one day I would be able to do a production of Shakespeare's *Merchant* in which that's the way it would happen, and I discussed this with Ewan Hooper one day. He said, 'That's very interesting, but you'd have to do a lot of rewriting'. I thought about it, and realized it would be simpler to write a new play.

Wesker, interviewed in *Theatre Quarterly,* 28 (1977), p.21

The portrayal of Shylock offends for being a lie about the Jewish character. I seek no pound of flesh but, like Shylock, I'm unforgiving, unforgiving of the play's contribution to the world's astigmatic view and murderous hatred of the Jew. . . . My first note to myself was that Shylock and Antonio must be friends. My second was that Shylock must be a bibliophile. Gradually, as I researched the history of the Venetian Empire, of the Jews in Italy, of the development of printing − of the entire Renaissance, in fact − I realized that my play would not be about bonds for usury but about bonds of friendship and the state laws which could threaten that friendship.

Wesker, *The Guardian,* 20 Aug. 1981

One More Ride on the Merry-Go-Round

Comedy in two acts.
Written: 1978.
Unperformed.
Unpublished.

Jasper and Nita have broken from a stifling marriage, in which each blames the other for lacking excitement and passion. Jasper is also celebrating his fiftieth birthday and the loss of his university lectureship: his girl-friend Monica and three bitchy ex-colleagues discuss the justification of the work ethic without convincing him. Nita, fulfilled in her work and relationship with her boy-friend Matt, cannot convince daughter Christine of the necessity of a profession, until a deus ex machina, a German conjurer, arrives, reveals that he is an unknown, illegitimate son of Jasper, and inspires Christine with a vocation to be a magician's assistant. She, like Jasper, plans to escape from the world of professions and ethics into a nomadic and bohemian existence.

Now I think Peter Hall's observation [about the play] is correct. By 'not centred' he means that the play has not quite made up its mind what it's about. This is because I simply set out to write something funny. In the process two themes shadowily emerged through which I plied the fun. Nothing wrong with these two themes providing one is the stronger, becomes the central drive. In *Merry-Go-Round* this doesn't seem to have happened. Is it about the way in which a couple blossom into what each wants the other to be only when they have separated? Or is it about the demise of the work ethic?

Wesker, diary entry quoted in Leeming, *Wesker the Playwright*

Caritas

Play in two acts.
Written: 1980.
First production: 7 Oct. 1981, Cottesloe Th. at the National
   Th., London (dir. John Madden; des. Andrew Jackness;
   with Patti Love as Christine).
Published: London: Cape, 1981.

Set in fourteenth-century Norfolk, it opens with the final moments of Christine Carpenter's (Patti Love) voluntary withdrawal from the 'kingdom of the world' into the cloistered solitude of a windowless cell where she will stay the rest of her life. For the first half we only hear her – imploring, ranting as though possessed, or just weeping with pleasure and fear.... Christine's mind turns, and she sees that she is not 'called', the set reverses. Now we look into the cell and can only hear her inter- locutors. She begs for release from her vows, but the bishop (Frederick Treves) refuses: for the nun as for the serf, duty must be endured. Christine is thus driven mad, and we are left with the image of her rocking to and fro manically chanting meaningless catechisms.

This conflict is framed by the Peasants' Revolt, led by Wat Tyler, of which we hear inklings.... The overall picture is of a people befuddled and cramped by organized religion. Within this Wesker works by counter-position rather than conflict. Though there is much argument in the dialogue, the effect is somehow abstract, as though the underlying social condition of the charac- ters is not being grappled with.

The consequence is that *Caritas* has the feel of a modern morality play. Unfortunately John Madden's production obscures this. The minimalist lighting and bleak sets erase all contrasts in the production, and so the drama that Wesker wrote is bypassed and the compulsiveness of a morality play is missed.

Michael Stewart, *Tribune,* 30 Oct. 1981

I don't want to enter into the psychology of the act or the girl. Something in the nature of the act — consisting as it does of retreat, self-sacrifice, and suffering — is there in us all. I simply want to create an archetypal story. In simple steps. With as little sophistry exchanged as possible. The decision, the act itself, is so powerful that it carries its own resonance.

Wesker, diary entry, quoted in Leeming, *Wesker the Playwright*

Sullied Hands

Comedy in one act.
Written: 1981.
Unperformed.
Unpublished:

Malcolm takes each of the guests at his dinner party into the large luxurious lavatory. Only gradually is it revealed that he has inven-

ted a dispenser for disinfected hand-wiping tissues which he expects to make him a millionaire, and is investigating consumer demand from his guests. The guinea-pigs' embarrassment and their various in-loo rituals create the comedy of the play.

Annie Wobbler

'Three monologues for my friend Nichola McAuliffe.'
Written: 1980-81.
First production: under the title *Annie, Anna, Annabella,*
    Suddeutscher Rundfunk, 3 Feb. 1983.
First British production: Birmingham Repertory Th. Studio, 5
    July 1983 (dir. Wesker; des. Pamela Howard; with Nichola
    McAuliffe as all three women), trans. to New End Theatre,
    London, 26 July 1983.
Revived: Fortune Th., London, 13 Nov. 1984.

Three quite separate characters are revealed in monologue. Annie Wobbler is an old charwoman-turned-tramp, reminiscing vaguely about her days in 'service'. Anna is a beautiful young woman, newly graduated, assessing her intelligence, personality, and relationship with the world as she dresses to go out. Annabella is a successful novelist, whose monologue is again divided into three, being three alternative interview-persona she assumes — in turn aggressive, provocatively vague, and honestly bewildered.

The middle sketch is a pure treat, with McAuliffe at her most delicious. A Cambridge graduate prepares for her date, painstakingly applying the makeup he loathes, gradually revealing with graceful and grinning glee what a duffer he is. . . . A free-spirited two fingers to the rest of the world because she feels great and no one . . . is going to spoil her fun.
                    Susie McKenzie, *Time Out*, 4-10 Aug. 1983

All three different characters are shown with an intensity of personal involvement which is where Mr. Wesker flourishes best.
                    Rosemary Say, *Sunday Telegraph*, 31 July 1983

No disrespect to Mr. Wesker, who directs like a director, but he shouldn't have to be doodling like this. The author of half a dozen of the more interesting plays of our era is still, very much, with us.

Giles Gordon, The Spectator, 5 Aug. 1983

Annie Wobbler is one of a series of East End sketches which I began in Aug. 1949. Her image has remained with me. In writing this homage to a childhood memory I've also recreated a memory of childhood. When I sat down to write the monologue I did not have an actress in mind. For reasons I can't remember I was unable to move beyond the first page. In the spring of 1980 Birmingham Repertory Theatre were auditioning for *The Wedding Feast*. Peter Farago, the director re-called an actress who'd impressed him. She impressed me. I went to see her in Stewart Parker's *Catchpenny Twist* at the Kings Head. Her power was unmistakeable. In *The Wedding Feast* she confirmed it.

I'd never written for an actress before, nor written for a solo voice. A year later, after my abortive beginning those unpredictable writing juices flowed again. With Nichola in mind I was able to complete *Annie Wobbler*. Anna was directly inspired by the personality of Nichola, though it is by no means a biographical study. Annabella grew out of a note I'd made of something said by Judith Rosner whose novel *Waiting for Mr. Godber* had just been made into a film. By the end of 1981 I was able to send Nichola the script as a Christmas present . . .

No relationship between these character studies is intended. Each has a life of her own. What I hope will be felt is a poetic relationship. There but for the grace, or wrath, of God go each one. Or, as a critic succinctly put it: 'Three wobbly egos defiantly asserting themselves.'

Wesker, programme note, 1983

Mothers

'Four portraits on the theme of the mother.'
Written: 1982.
First performance: Matzukoshi Royal Th., Tokyo, 2 July 1982
    (dir. Tsunetoshi Hirowtari; with Michiko Ohtsuka as the
    mothers).

Four successive views of the mother – as aunt or as substitute non-mother, as struggling single parent, as failure, and as failed fulfilled mother.

44

Menace

Play for television.
Written: 1961.
First transmitted: BBC Television, 8 Dec. 1963 (dir.
    Herbert Wise; with Joanna Dunham as Harriet, John
    Hurt as Gerry, and Patience Collier as Sophie).
Published: *Jewish Quarterly,* July 1963; *revised version*:
    in *Six Sundays in January* (London: Cape, 1971).

Menace – *Arnold Wesker's first play to be specially
written for television . . . dealt with an evening in the
lives of lonely and frustrated people, living their separate
lives in separate rooms. . . . Gradually we see that what
menaces these people is the society in which we live. . . .
The final scene where the two young people joined in a
folk dance was a moment of delight, a release from
tension and symbolic in the joined hands and circle
formation of the dance of the hope that comes from
unity.*

Daily Worker, 14 Dec. 1963

Love Letters on Blue Paper

Play for television.
Written: 1975, adapted from his short story of the same
    title.
First transmitted: 2 Mar. 1976 (dir. Waris Hussein; with
    Elizabeth Spriggs as Sonia, Patrick Troughton as
    Victor, and Richard Pasco as Maurice).
Published only in stage version (see p.35): London: TQ
    Publications, 1978 (New Plays series); and in *Wesker, 3.*

Love Letters . . . *began life as a short story and is essen-
tially two parallel speeches: a dying man talking about
his dread of death and his wife passionately asserting her
love. They do not talk to each other at all. He confides
in a friend, she pours out her adoration in letters and
posts them to him. It is rather like the dying Keats listen-
ing to the nightingale.*

She comforts him with huge pillows like breasts, she stays him with strawberry jam and cream, and, as he grows weaker, her song grows stronger. As he dies of leukaemia she is singing like a bird: 'Your blood in my blood, rivers of it. Do you know it? Do you?'

It gains everything from being heard and little, I think, from being seen. The device of the narrator looks odd. . . . The device of handing the letters over to the narrator because someone must read them never begins to look right. . . . But I thought it was triumphant. Not triumphantly successful as a play. Just triumphant, as in trumpets.

Nancy Banks-Smith, *The Guardian,* 3 Mar. 1976

Whitsun

Television play.
*Written:*1980, adapted from his short story 'The Visit'.
Unperformed.
Unpublished.

A Danish couple are living in Cambridgeshire. He's doing post-graduate research, she's a social worker, and they have marital problems. One hot Whitsun they are visited by slightly older English friends, a former professor of art history and his wife. They eat breakfast in the garden, go for cycle rides, listen to music, eat out, talk, play games. Finally the friendship seems to help the younger couple's problems.

Breakfast

Television play.
Unperformed.
Unpublished.

An English Jew visits Germany on business, and enjoys the hospitality, cleanliness, and food, especially breakfast. Though reading a paperback on the Jews in the concentration camps, he refuses to become emotional about the war, as he explains to a guilt-ridden German business acquaintance. Yet the play ends with his involuntary tears, while reading, during breakfast.

a : Fiction

Collections
referred to by short titles below and elsewhere.

Six Sundays in January. London: Cape, 1971. Referred
to as *SS*.

Love Letters on Blue Paper. London: Cape, 1974.
Referred to as *LL*.

Said the Old Man to the Young Man. London: Cape,
1978. Referred to as *SOM*.

Love Letters on Blue Paper, and Other Stories. London:
Penguin, 1980. Referred to as *LLOS*.

Individual Stories
'Pools', *Jewish Quarterly*, IV, 2; also in *SS*.

'Six Sundays in January', *Jewish Quarterly*, XVII, 2;
also in *SS* and *LLOS*.

'The Man Who Became Afraid'; in *LL* and *LLOS*.

'A Time of Dying'; in *LL*.

'Love Letters on Blue Paper'; in *LL* and *LLOS*.

Say Goodbye! You May Never See them Again (text
to accompany a book of paintings by John Allen).
London: Cape, 1974.

'The Man Who Would Never Write Like Balzac', *Jewish
Quarterly*, XXIII, 1 and 2; also in *SOM*.

Fatlips: a Story for Young People (illustrated by Oscar
Zarete). London: Writers and Readers Cooperative;
New York: Harper and Row, 1978.

'Said the Old Man to the Young Man'; in *SOM*.

'The Visit'; in *SOM* and *LLOS*.

Poems
'The Poor', *Plan*, March 1952.

'Time Parts the Memory', *Jewish Quarterly*, Winter
1959-60.

'The Book in my Hand', *Overland* (Melbourne), 18 (1960).

'My Child', *Overland* (Melbourne), 19 (1960); also in
The Sixties, Spring 1961.

'I Walk the Streets of Norwich', *Konkret* (Hamburg),
20 (October 1961).

'Sitting Waiting for Auntie Anne', *Stepney Words, 2*
(1971).

'You Love Me Now', *Contrasts* (Shiplake College), 1972.
'Sebastian', in Spike Milligan and Jack Hobbs, eds., *Milligan's Ark* (London: M. and J. Hobbs, 1977).
'It was a Time of Feast and Weddings', *Piano,* Opus 1, (Washington DC: Pushkin Press, July 1978).
'Poem' and 'Chariot and Chair', *Jewish Chronicle,* 22 June 1981.
'All My Years Before Me', *Jewish Chronicle,* 21 Dec. 1981.
'All Things Tire of Themselves', *Jewish Chronicle,* 17 May 1982.

Personal Experience and Art

I have attempted many times to talk with myself and ask why and how. But I know that I forget . . . in fact, one forgets all the books that one reads, and I have got a terrible memory, anyway. So that sometimes I express an opinion and forget the justification for it, and the reason why it's part of me: but it didn't form entirely out of the air, it formed because of so many things that have happened, and books that I have read. But I forget. . . . And then there's another explanation of my writing plays, which is that they are attempts to continue arguments that I have had with friends and relatives and people that I worked with. . . . The plays continue human relationships as well as arguments – relationships that have gone wrong – and the pause that art gives you is the opportunity to rectify those relationships or explain them. . . . Sarah Kahn in *Chicken Soup* is a member of the Communist Party, and my mother is a member of the Communist Party. Beatie Bryant in *Roots* is the daughter of farm labourers in Norfolk, and my wife is the daughter of farm labourers in Norfolk. Dave in *Jerusalem,* who went to live and work in the country, can obviously be compared to my own sister and brother-in-law, who did the same thing. But these are the obvious relationships. What isn't obvious is what I choose to select and juxtapose and extend. I married my wife: Ronnie in *Roots* does not. Now, knowing that Ronnie doesn't – and that there are many kinds of Ronnies, who never face up to the final challenge of their own beliefs or instincts – altered the details and the shape of the whole play. So this is where the imaginative quality comes into my writing, as opposed to the recreation of facts and incidents.

Theatre at Work, p.78-80

It seems to me that there are two ways in which an artist can approach his work. One, for want of a better word, is an intellectual approach – that is to say, to begin with a concept, with a theme, an idea which the artist wants to explore in a play or a novel, and then to look round for situations or characters to flesh it out. Other artists begin with experience. At the climax of a certain kind of experience, they suddenly burst and feel that they must organize it in the form of a play, a poem, or a novel. Both of these approaches have produced very great works of art, but I would hazard a guess that the very greatest works of literature are those that spring from experience — they have the quality of guts and urgency and inevitability. You feel this inexorable drive of experience in the work — it couldn't be any other way. Which is not to say that my plays are great works of art, but to describe the way I work.

Theatre Quarterly, 28 (1977), p.5-6

The problem in reading about Christian mystics is that I experience a constant criticism of my own life. It's unsettling in that my imperfections are shown me through a view of the universe I can't accept. On the other hand why shouldn't I recognize that good and evil struggle in me in the form of good acts (neither good nor frequent enough) compensating for — what? Not evil acts. I'm not that surely? No, the normal sins of pride, wrath, carnality. I once thought I had mystical tendencies. I see mysticism now as a tendency to make things conveniently fit — a need in all men which emerges in different cultures in different ways at different times. No — that's a shallow observation.

But no sound or sight of the play yet. Too soon. . . . Think one of the reasons I waste time writing this diary (if I haven't already said this) is that I imagine the random record will, in its final totality, make a sense that I can't make of moment to moment.

Unpublished diary, on the writing of *Caritas*

On 'Realism' in Art
Well, definitions. I think that realistic art is a contradiction in terms, it doesn't exist, it's an impossibility, because reality is quite obviously every minute detail. What I do believe is that all art deals with reality, whether it's the reality of actual experience or imaginative experience — and this includes fantasy, and the dream and so on — but it deals with it in different ways: it deals with it naturalistically, stylistically, surrealistically. . . . And with that in mind, *The Kitchen* is really what *Chips* is, a kind of stylized naturalism. Whereas the Trilogy is less stylized naturalism, although contained within that concept, the notion of stylization, is a whole notion of art, of artifice. *The Kitchen* is more stylized than *Chicken Soup,* and *Chips* more stylized even than *The Kitchen.*

Theatre at Work, p.89

There appears to exist a need on the part of critics and audience to place an artist's work beneath columns neatly headed with labels. The need exists, I think, because it's felt that the labelling will help them *understand* the artist's work. . . . The need is understandable but the labels supplied are often unhelpful, distorting. I'd like you for a moment to forget all such categorizing and to consider instead the following observation as possibly a more helpful and — to my mind — more accurate guide to the understanding of an artist's work.

No art is realistic. The concept of 'realistic' art is a concept involving contradictions. No play or story I've ever written can be usefully or truthfully described as a realistic play or story. The recreation of total reality in any artistic medium is impossible. It's even impossible to *experience* total reality, reality being the sum total of so many different elements. . . . However, although there is no such phenomenon as realistic art, it *is* quite interesting and helpful to observe that all art *deals* with the experience of reality. . . . We can now say an artist is dealing with what is absurd in reality, or what is paradoxical in reality, or ironic or mystical or commanding of our pity. And we may add that the artist is dealing with what is absurd in reality in a naturalistic form, as Pinter sometimes does, or he's dealing with naturalistic aspects of reality in an absurd form, which is what is happening I think in Beckett's *Godot*. . . . It means nothing to think of my plays and stories as social realism — a term I've always resented because it blinded people to those other elements in my work I'd always hoped would be recognized: the paradoxical, the lyrical, the absurd, ironic, musical, farcical, and so on; all the elements united, as Ruskin says, in 'due place and measure'.

Unpublished lecture

Art as Selection

I feel driven to discover for myself my true role. It is, I think, an ability to take hold of one of those secondary truths about life — never an originally discovered one, or rather I may have discovered it for myself but others were there before me — and to illustrate it. If I have any talent it is for selecting and arranging from among the right elements those which will illustrate that truth. I say 'from among' because there are many elements which could illustrate it, and I chose those to which *I* respond, which say more, seem more right to *me*. Other playwrights reach out for others among those elements. Bad playwrights miss the pile altogether and select from the wrong or inconsequential elements.

Instinct and intellect mix to make the choice. So — I know the simple, secondary truth that an idea can possess and imprison the free and generous spirit of a person. *Caritas* aims to illustrate that. It's a modest talent but I bring to it the power of concentration and seriousness and what perception I have, and the skill of a craft. And that is all I can do. If poetry touches the work, I'm pleased. It's something. And I must hold on to it.

Unpublished diary, on the writing of *Caritas*

Dialogue and Rhythm

At the time [1957] I was concerned with language, and I'd worked out of myself the more naturalistic dialogue. I was no longer satisfied with the colloquialisms and ordinary rhythms of everyday speech, but wanted somehow to find a heightened language, which had to avoid being pretentious and pseudo-poetic, but which was nevertheless a valid manipulation of language. . . . I always get annoyed with critics who talk about me being a 'master of dialogue'. Well, for Christ's sake, if you're not a master of that, what else? This is only the beginning and should be the reason why a play is good, it's the least that one expects. . . . I think, in as far as I have a facility for writing dialogue, it is because I am conscious of speech-rhythms, and so instinctively I will write them in the way they should be. I think I developed more self-consciousness about this, and then began deliberately to work out the rhythms so that the Smiler speech [in *Chips*] has more definitive rhythm in it. But in that it can be spoken, it does seem natural, and is perhaps true.

Theatre at Work, p.88-91

In Writing [*The Four Seasons*] I confronted one other major problem: how to avoid the trap of creating a pseudo-poetic dialogue. . . . The words and rhythms of everyday speech are rich and contain their own poetry, but after a time they cease to be adequate. In six plays (*Their Very Own and Golden City* was written before *The Four Seasons*) I had wrung from such speech rhythms all that I was able, at least for the moment, and wanted to create a heightened and lyrical language. Of course pretentiousness had to be avoided, but the problem of using current English dialogue lay in its impoverishment; it is a real and disturbing problem.

'Epilogue' to *The Four Seasons,* in *Wesker,* 2, p.118

An author sometimes spends hours balancing six sentences in a monologue to ensure: (1) they belong to the character uttering them; (2) they have an intellectual or emotional dynamic that is both compelling and valid; (3) they have rhythm; (4) they appear at the right and inevitable point in the scene; and so on. Sometimes he achieves all this instinctively and without effort, but usually the reasons or instincts he's brought to bear in the achievement are, odd though it may sound, often forgotten.

'The Playwright as Director', *Plays and Players,*
February 1974, p.12

The Nature of Artistic Development

It cannot be claimed that the greater degree of technical sophistication has made a significant difference to the quality of theatre writing. I doubt if the mere existence of the magnificent National Theatre will produce a Shakespeare! Besides, even the elements in the structure of text have remained the same: there has been verse, lyrical prose, lyrical naturalism, colloquial and absurd dialogue. Each writer in a generation or wave may have learned how to respond to the texture, sound, and rhythmic needs of the day, but does any such response signify 'development'? A tuned ear is the basic tool we expect in a writer. . . . Or should we look to the framework within which the text lives? But that, likewise, has been thoroughly explored. . . . To move from a traditional three-act drama to a multi-scened one may involve a degree of courage, but can that be described as 'development'? Isn't that rather 'rearrangement'? The playwright may have found the courage to take on more complex *technical* challenges, but he may be applying that complex structure to say the same things. The technical flurries may be very intoxicating and thrilling in themselves but they can very easily be hiding a trite or uninteresting observation about human behaviour. . . . When one has broken a work into its physical parts . . . then one other and final element needs to be added: the artist's perception. It's a very difficult element to discuss — being made up of many intangibles. But I'd like to look at my own work and try to indicate what I mean by development and show how I'd like to think my plays have developed.

As a playwright I'm mostly of the school which begins with experience rather than ideas. I'm not a writer who illustrates ideas, or explores ideas through invented characters and situations; rather I'm a writer whose experience drives me to organize that experience into a play or story because it seems to illuminate to me some aspect of human behaviour. There are some exceptions to this, but it's generally true enough to be worth observing. So the plays I'd like to refer to are my first play *The Kitchen* and a play written twelve years later — *The Journalists*. Both are attempts to organize experience.

They both have other things in common as well, the form and the setting. Both have a large cast of about 30, who are on stage most of the time, and both are set in a place of work: the kitchen of a huge restaurant; the offices of a large Sunday newspaper. They also have similar rhythms — *The Kitchen* begins with the chefs and waitresses slowly ambling into an empty space and preparing for a frenzied serving as the day reaches its climax. *The Journalists* begins at the beginning of the week and slowly moves towards the frenzied activity on a Saturday when the paper is being put to bed. In both we see people working and in both we glance in on their private lives and fears and attitudes. But here the similarities end.

There are two main differences. The first is that although both are based on experiences, yet the experiencing was different. I actually worked for four years in kitchens — moving up from kitchen-porter to pastry-chef, whereas I'd never *worked* as a journalist; I'd only experienced journalism through reading newspapers in general and suffering personal interviews and reviews in particular, and had spent two months in the offices of *The Sunday Times* to obtain background material and knowledge of work methods.

The second difference is between the themes of the two plays. Whereas my experience of the kitchen produced the theme of the relationship of people to their work, my experience of journalism produced a much more complex theme: the relationship between the Lilliputian mentality and a certain concept of democracy — a very difficult and dangerous thought — especially for someone who imagined himself to be a democratic socialist . . . signs of this are there in that very first play — *The Kitchen:* [for example, in Paul's long story about the bus-driver]. Now, that's the longest and only monologue there is in the play. For the rest, it's all trivial exchange and the actions of a kitchen . . . . Of course I like the play and think it's effective, and it seems to work as a powerful image all around: the employer is bewildered by what happens and says I give you plenty of work, good wages, you eat all you want — what more is there? The question is potent, potent but simple. The action leading up to it is theatrically thrilling, but there is no one around with a mind or imagination of any quality to shape the action at a more profound level, or to react to Lilliputianism at a more profound level. With *The Journalists* there seemed to be more of an opportunity to do this. . . . Twelve years on I was looking for Lilliputians in much loftier places than the ranks of poor be-leaguered bus-drivers. . . .

I think you'll see from this that what I'm trying to say is that part of the nature of true development in a playwright — or any artist — is to do with the greater complexity of experience they tackle and the more challenging thoughts they offer for consideration. It is not to do with form: the form of my very first play engaged over 30 actors simulating work and all on stage at the same time — as complex and daring (or foolhardy) to handle as the play twelve years later. . . .

In case any of you were beginning to think I was saying simply that if an artist becomes cleverer, even wiser, it was sufficient — I wasn't. I'm not. No, a more thoughtful artist *is* desirable if there's to be any development, but something in addition to thoughtfulness is needed: a sharper poetic sense. . . . In constructing *The Journalists* I was very aware of two things: the rhythm which could be created by moving from department to department. It could not be arbitrary. The time spent in each place had to be the correct length, not too long, not too short. And I was also aware of the special effect which could be created by juxtaposing one issue alongside another. That special effect, that juxtapositioning, is what I call poetry in the theatre, and it's indefinable. You can only place two passages alongside one another and trust it works for an audience, rather like editing a film and placing two images alongside each other so that, though unrelated, yet they intensify each other, then that's what I think can be called poetic.

Unpublished lecture, 'The Nature of Development'

The Writing Process

My procedure was — and still is — to write it out in longhand, leave it alone for a while, and then go back over the longhand. Because of the alterations one makes on the longhand draft, it becomes cluttered with words, and you can't really see it. So it then becomes what I call the first typed draft. Then I go over that, and produce the final draft. *Golden City,* however, has just gone on and on and on, and we have really eight drafts of one kind or another.

Theatre at Work, p.82

I actually began writing [*The Friends*] on 20 January 1967 . . .
I'm still adding notes to the written draft in June 1968 – good
god, that's a year and a half afterwards. . . . I think the play
begins with very personal thoughts, which grow and grow inside
one. And inside this a shape begins to present itself. I find I just
live in the atmosphere of it. I felt this with *The Friends*. I felt it
very strongly with *Love Letters on Blue Paper*, and with *The
Merchant*. . .

It never occurs to me that the notes I'm making suggest that
this has got to be in three acts over 24 hours, or in 50 scenes
over 50 years. I think that the shape comes, almost instinctively,
with the material. When I knew I wanted to write *The Four
Seasons*, I didn't say, ah, now I must divide this into four acts.
It could have been in some other form, but the way in which it
was eventually written just emerged from the material. . . .

The successive drafts don't usually effect the structure, but are
more in the way of polishing. Though parts of the polishing take
in, I suspect, some of the structure. *The Friends*, though, always
took place in one 24-hour period – it was never a week condensed
into 24 hours. And *The Kitchen* was always conceived as 'a day
in the life of' – whereas it could have been three mornings.
Chips was always the eight weeks of the square-bashing period.
Golden City was always from 1928 to 1990. And so on. I might
rearrange scenes, but I regard that as part of the polishing. And I
might have given the wrong dialogue to the wrong characters. Or
have got the rhythm wrong. And getting things like those right is
all part of the act of polishing, but it couldn't be called changing
the overall shape.

Theatre Quarterly, 28 (1977), p.7-8

Last night [21 June 1980] I started on [*Caritas*]. More or less. A
speech and a bit. The truth is, I'm now going through the three
books of notes I've been making, to refresh my poor memory.
There is so much fascinating history to be resisted. . . .

[22 June] It's hard, this one. Finished reading my notebooks.
The notes on history held me more than the notebook of
dialogue. Almost feel like I did that night here I read the first
pages I'd written of *The Merchant* and wanted to flee. I feel so
unfit for it. How can I become a fourteenth-century person? On
the other hand, to what extent do I need to? I sense and don't
sense the play. It swims to me, then away from me. The opening
scene of the ritual was easy, simply had to précis a book of
instructions. But afterwards, I'm like a man confronted with a

treasure chest I don't know how to open. I turn it this way and that, prise it here a little and find I've damaged it, push it there a little and find it shifts. I tickle it, heave it, stare at it, finger the patterns, turn it round and round, never certain that I'm the one to open it. . . .

[23 June] Wrote two scenes, finally, yesterday. But it hasn't taken off. Feel that if I get something down I will have something to look at, some paths to walk along. I know what I'm after, but not if I'm achieving it.

[24 June] As the day came to an end, around nine to eleven o'clock yesterday, I squeezed out two scenes! Seems I take all day to breathe in, and let it out in the last minutes! But I've no idea how it's shaping. A first scene is one thing, when a second is added it becomes different again, and so on. I've no sense, yet, what the six-scened creature in my black book is like.

Later: Extraordinary experience! I've nearly got on top of it! The day frittered away . . . came to study to attack play. Reread what had been written, not too bad. A shape and atmosphere. Then wrote a new scene − mostly based on notes − and I knew last night it was the one I was going to continue with today, so it was not difficult. And it seemed to me I could see the next scene, and from then on the next two. Suddenly I had a sense of flow, a sense of juices at work in me. Felt confident, that I could take my time now. Saw some sheep had escaped from one field into a next. . . . Returned and reached out to pick up the rhythm again, but it was gone. I've sat from about eight-thirty till eleven, head clasped in hands, or staring into space, or eyes closed, and I could make nothing come together. How could I lose something that seemed so certain? That was *there*?. . .

[5 July] Have just finished Act One. It fell into place. Sixteen short scenes − most of them short, anyway. It's only a first draft and I know of at least one scene which doesn't work − Scene 10. But of course there's an enormous amount of work to be done on all of them. . . .

[7 July] It is mad − but I've finished the play! Of course only the first draft but − something is down on paper. I began a little of Act Two on Sunday and wrote seven and a half pages today. Much was already there in my notebook and my head. I had simply to arrange it. Act Two is the strangest piece of writing I've ever committed to paper. It's a collection of moments divided by chants. . . . A collection of moments, that's the best description. Are they the right moments, though? And does such a collection work, anyway?

English critics will really hate this one.

But it's done. Ha! Ha! A first draft. Now I can concentrate on the really important work of getting my garden in order! (Oh, I do dread reading it. Will leave that for a couple of days — or more.) . . .

[16 July] I started to read the play, but it was impossible, my manuscript is so covered in crossings out and arrows that go this way, then that way. I had to start typing it in order that I could see it properly. I've typed the first draft, making changes as I went along, and I'm horrified to find it may be much longer than I thought. I felt I'd written a nice short brilliant work. It's the second act which is short. The first act is about 35 pages. The second only eight!!! Damn! It's like building a boat and then pushing it out into the sea to discover the water comes up over the port-holes on to the deck! If I don't release some over-weight it'll sink. . . .

[17 July] I suddenly had the idea to take out the concept of two Gods from the first act and have [Christine] seen discovering it, and then have the Bishop and Matthew inquisition her, in the early middle of the second act, thus breaking up her one-woman act — though I did like that. . . .

[28 July] Forced myself to work on *Caritas* last night. Transferred the corrections to the carbon copy preparing it for the typewriting agency, Scripts Ltd. A mechanical job. . . .

[20 August] So — here we go again. Responses from friends, positive, next the humiliating battle to get it on. Then the depressing critics.

Unpublished diary, on writing *Caritas*

The Jew as a Free Spirit

The Merchant is an original play — *not* in verse — based on the same three stories which Shakespeare used for his play *The Merchant of Venice*. Maurice Sarrazin (one of France's foremost actors and also, since 1945, the director of the Grenier de Toulouse in France) felt there was therefore no surprise in my play. . . . Finally he asked: 'In a word what is your Shylock about?' . . . I'd never thought of him in a word. Being a vain playwright I'd always imagined my Shylock to be arrestingly complex, too contradictory to be held down by one word or phrase. But we were both rather excited by this time and my adrenalin was flowing and suddenly it came to me: my Shylock was a free spirit. That's what he was about, and that's what I was about, and that, I realized, is what Jewishness is about. . . .

But . . . from a play whose characters are not Jewish, to one of my latest plays: *Caritas*. . . . It is about a fourteenth-century anchoress called Christine Carpenter. . . . Christine, as I've understood her, was born a free spirit, she thought she wanted to be free of the body's needs and demands so that she could fly away to God. In the end, as she's slowly going mad, she reveals that what she really wanted was to be free to live a very human life. . . . [Then in *The Merchant*] Shylock, the foolish, defiant free spirit! He irritates on two levels: he neither conforms to what is expected of him outside by a public brought up on Shakespeare's image of him; nor will he do what he is told within the play. Shakespeare's Shylock on the other hand is a very well behaved Jew, he behaves as is expected of him. He is malevolent from the start. . . . The gentile world feels very comfortable with such a portrait. It conforms to the image of the Jew which most reassures them. . . .

My Shylock, on the other hand, is distressing in another way. To begin with, he is so clever that he can conduct his money-lending and warehousing with only a corner of his attention, the rest he devotes to his real passion: book collecting! Who does he think he is? Worse! He refuses to accept the constricting spiritual as well as physical walls of the Ghetto, and claims a Christian for a friend. Who does he think he is?. . . He invents a mocking bond for a pound of flesh. He wants to mock them! Who does he think he is? And he's arrogant with it all. Not only does he talk to Antonio as an equal but he's contemptuous of Antonio's young guests, especially the fanatical Lorenzo, with whom he refuses to engage in debate; and when he does, he tells *them* how to read the history of *their* own state! Really, who does he think he is?

But perhaps the greatest offence is that he refuses to accept the generosity of Lorenzo who tries to draw the court away from an anti-semitic stance by eulogizing the virtues of Jews who are — and here Lorenzo borrows the lines Shakespeare gave to Shylock — fed with the same food, hurt with the same weapons, subject to the same diseases, and so on and so forth. All of which patronizing infuriates the unappreciative, stiff-necked Shylock. . . . What ingratitude! He wants no special pleading? His humanity is his right? He won't accept the graciously bestowed privilege of being apologised for? Who does this dreadful man think he is?

Well, we know who he thinks he is. Foolishly, he thinks he's a free spirit, and irritatingly he behaves like one. . . . The free spirit implies the supremacy of the human being over the state, over repressive authority, over that which aims to frustrate initiative, cripple imagination, induce conformity. Shylock embodies all of this: in his friendship, his passion for books, in his contempt for a racialist law, in the way he reads history.

Amazing! Knowledge, like underground springs, fresh and constantly there, till one day — up! Bubbling! For dying men to drink.

Upon which my case rests.

Unpublished lecture, 'The Two Roots of Judaism'

On Actors and Directors

I'm not only dependent on actors for actually performing a play, but for confirming the way I have seen the characters and the logic and the rhythm within which I have set them. An example which I've often quoted is Joan Plowright's contribution to *Roots*. She said that a whole half-page in the third act belonged in the second act: she was right, and it was shifted — and she contributed all sorts of minor bits of dialogue, which I can't remember. . . .

I don't know whether there exists a language to describe the position of the actor *vis à vis* the character, as opposed to the author. It is a question of the internal and the external: when you're actually having to say the lines and you are aware of the physical situation and what has come before and what is to come later, the words are comfortable or they're not, and only an actor knows it — a way of measuring how good an author is, the extent to which everything he's written allows an actor to feel comfortable. . . .

I not only can but need to work with actors in this way. What I'm not able to do is collaborate with actors in working out *what* I want to say. And although there have been productions which have employed that method of work between actors and author, and which have produced interesting results, I finally believe it is not a way in which good work can generally be done. Because it demands compromise, and although compromise is necessary in all fields of human activity, it seems to me that art is the last place where it should be required to occur, be demanded and expected. And for that reason I cannot work in a co-operative way to arrive at the final script, the final concept. But to co-operate with actors in finding the best production approach to that conception, yes, that's natural, and inherent in theatre anyway.

Theatre Quarterly, 28 (1977), p.16

The arguments against the playwright directing his own play seem to go like this: (1) The dramatist cannot be objective about his work. . . . (2) The playwright only *writes* the play: he has no appreciation of the technical problems involved in mounting it – 'What works on the desk is one thing, the stage is another'. (3) Actors are inhibited in front of the writer and cannot experiment. . . . Having attended the rehearsals of all ten of my plays on stage, four again on TV, one again in the film studio, and having directed five of them myself – one in England, unhappily, and four abroad – I'm in a position to comment on these objections which are, except for one, most curious.

One: Objectivity is presumably the ability to detach oneself. . . . It's not unreasonable that a certain moment is reached – by most playwrights – when they've used up the present supply of 'objectivity' and require recharging by an opinion authoritatively founded in theatrical experience – a director's, a set-designer's. For this reason I also owe certain changes in my plays to John Dexter. But, and here is the interesting point, though changes were made to *The Old Ones* under Dexter's direction in London, yet other changes were made to the play under my own direction in Munich. The conclusion could be that it is the *possibility* for change which encourages change, not the person. Give an author the chance to direct his own play and he will change as crisply and perceptively as any director. . . .

Two: The best playwrights make not impossible but unfamiliar demands upon the theatre, they stretch its preconceived limitations. If the desk *is* one thing and the stage another, then all the more reason for a playwright to come closer to his material.

Three: The actor/director relationship touches upon what is central to all productions . . . the responsibility, for guiding an actor and helping him shape the performance in which he will not make a fool of himself, is an awful one. In taking on directorship the author divides his loyalties between a responsibility to his play and a responsibility to his actors. . . .

My argument is this: there is no mystique inherent in the craft of directing, the craft can be learnt. The learning may not make a great director, but *it can be learnt*. And if the author has the wish, the inclination, the patience, he, like the director, can command the craft through experience. More, *if* it can be learnt then the combination of the two talents in the one man is formidable and, potentially, thrilling.

'The Playwright as Director', *Plays and Players,*
February 1974, p.11-14

a : Primary Sources

Collections of Plays
cited elsewhere by short titles, as below.

Wesker Trilogy: The Wesker Trilogy. London: Cape, 1960; New York: Random House, 1961; Penguin, 1964. [*Chicken Soup with Barley, Roots, I'm Talking about Jerusalem.*]

Wesker, 1: Arnold Wesker, Volume 1. Penguin, 1981. [Revised reprint of *The Wesker Trilogy.*]

Wesker, 2: Arnold Wesker, Volume 2. Penguin, 1981. [Revised reprint of *Three Plays* (Penguin, 1976), containing *The Kitchen, The Four Seasons, Their Very Own and Golden City.*]

Wesker, 3: Arnold Wesker, Volume 3. Penguin 1981. [*The Friends, The Old Ones, Love Letters on Blue Paper.*]

Wesker, 4. Arnold Wesker, Volume 4, Penguin, 1981. [*The Journalists, The Wedding Feast, The Merchant.*]

Articles, Essays, and Lectures

Collections

Fears of Fragmentation. London: Cape, 1970. [Referred to below as *FF.*]

The Journalists: a Triptych. London: Cape, 1979. [Referred to below as *Jat.*]

Individual Articles, Essays, and Lectures

'Let Battle Commence', *Encore* V, 4 (1958); also in Charles Marowitz, Tom Milne, and Owen Hale, eds., *The Encore Reader* (London: Methuen, 1965), reissued as *New Theatre Voices of the Fifties and Sixties* (London: Eyre Methuen, 1981).

'To React – to Respond', *Encore,* VI, 3 (1959).

'Two Lost Generations?', *Definition,* 1 (1960). [On audiences.]

'O Mother Is It Worth It?', published as a 'special' by *Gemini,* 1960; also in *FF.*

'Labour and the Arts', published as a 'special' by *Gemini,* 1960.

'Discovery', *Transatlantic Review,* Dec. 1960.

'Two Snarling Heads', lecture given in 1961; published in *FF.*

'Art is Not Enough', *Twentieth Century,* Feb. 1961.

'Resolution 42', *New Statesman,* Apr. 1961.

'The Secret Reins', *Encounter,* Mar. 1962; also published in *FF.*

'Art and Action', *The Listener,* 10 May 1962.

'After the Eichman Trial', *Jewish Quarterly,* XL, 1 (1962).

'False Gods: an Open Letter to Peter Brook', *Flourish* (RSC
    newspaper), 1966.

'The House', *Encounter,* Nov. 1966; as 'Tarnished Virtues and
    Confused Manners', published in *FF.*

'Delusions of Floral Grandeur', *Envoy,* Oct. 1967.

'Fears of Fragmentation', lecture given in 1968; published in *FF.*

'Casual Condemnations', *Theatre Quarterly,* I, 2 (1971).

'Last Letter to Aunt Sara', *The Garment Worker,* Oct. 1971.

'From a Writer's Notebook', *Theatre Quarterly,* II, 6 (1972).

'The Playwright's Boycott against Apartheid', *Contrast,* 29
    (1972).

'A Cretinue of Critics', *Drama,* Winter 1972. [Open letter to
    Harold Hobson on his review of *The Old Ones.*]

'Unhappy Poisons', *Plays and Players,* Nov. 1972. [Reply to John
    Russell Taylor's review of *The Old Ones.*]

'How to Cope with Criticism' [and a letter in the same issue],
    Plays and Players, Dec. 1972.

'East End My Cradle', *The Observer,* 24 Nov. 1974.

'The Playwright as Director', *Plays and Players,* Feb. 1974.

'Four Thoughts', *Plays and Players,* Oct. 1975.

'Each One a Landmark', in Frederick Raphael, ed., *Bookmarks*
    (London, 1975), p.154-61.

'Arnold Wesker', in Dom Moraes, ed., *Voices for Life* (New
    York, 1975), p.189-205.

'Critic at the Box-office', *The Observer,* 14 Mar. 1976.

Words – as Definitions of Experience. London: Readers and
    Writers Co-operative, 1976.

Journey into Jounalism. London: Readers and Writers
    Co-operative, 1977; also published in *Jat.*

'A Journal of *The Journalists', Theatre Quarterly,* VII, 26 (1977);
    also published in *Jat.*

'Debts to the Court', in Richard Findlater, ed, *At the Royal
    Court* (Ambergate: Amber Lane Press, 1981).

'Why I Fleshed out Shylock', *Guardian,* 29 Aug. 1981.

'The Strange Affair of the Actors' Revolt', *Sunday Times,* 30
    Aug. 1981.

'In Praise of Solitude', *Sunday Telegraph Magazine,* 24 Jan. 1982.

'Two Roots of Judaism', paper given at Rockefeller Conference, Sept. 1982.

'Excerpts from a New York Journal', in Ronald Harwood, ed., *A Night at the Theatre* (London, 1982), p.164-81. [Rehearsal diary for *The Merchant.*]

Interviews

Gerard Fay, 'Progress of a Young Playwright, *Manchester Guardian,* 6 August 1959.

Laurence Kitchin, 'Playwright to Watch', *Times,* 21 Sept. 1959; also in his *Mid-Century Drama* (Faber, 1960), p.194-6.

W.J. Weatherby, 'Breakfast with Wesker', *Manchester Guardian Weekly,* 18 Jan. 1960.

Robert Muller, 'Wesker', *Harpers Bazaar,* Oct. 1960.

Thomas Wiseman, 'The Aches and Pains of Wesker's Art', *Time and Tide,* 3 May 1962, p.21-2.

John Russell Taylor, *The Times,* 12 Dec. 1963.

Walter Wager, 'Interview with Arnold Wesker', *Playbill,* 1964; also in his *The Playwrights Speak* (New York: Delacourt Press; Harlow: Longman, 1968).

Simon Trussler, 'Interview with Arnold Wesker', *Tulane Drama Review,* XI, 2 (1966); also in Charles Marowitz and Simon Trussler, eds., *Theatre at Work* (London' Methuen, 1967; New York: Hill and Wang, 1968).

Geoffrey Sheridan, 'Mr. Wesker's Very Own and Gilded World', *Manchester Guardian Weekly,* 23 June 1966.

Ronald Hayman, in his *Arnold Wesker* (Heinemann, 1970).

Ronald Hayman, 'Arnold Wesker and John Dexter', *Transatlantic Review,* 48 (1973-74); also in his *Playback* 2 (Davis-Poynter, 1974).

Nigel Lewis, 'Interview with Arnold Wesker', *The Guardian,* 18 June 1974.

Karl-Heinz Stoll, 'Interviews with Edward Bond and Arnold Wesker', *Twentieth Century Literature,* XXII (1976), p.422-32.

Catherine Itzin, Glenda Leeming, and Simon Trussler, 'A Sense of What Should Follow', *Theatre Quarterly,* VII, 28 (1977).

Catherine Itzin, 'A Sense of Dread and Isolation', *Tribune,* 13 Oct. 1978.

'On Playwriting', *Performing Arts Journal,* II, 3 (Winter 1978), p.38-47.

Maureen Cleave, 'Interview with Arnold Wesker', *Observer Magazine,* 4 Oct. 1981.

b : Secondary Sources

Full-length Studies

Harold U. Ribalow, *Arnold Wesker.* New York: Twayne Publishers, 1965 (Twayne's English Author Series). [A superficial survey.]

Michael Marland, ed., *Arnold Wesker.* London: Times Education Services, 1970. [Fasimile collection of various articles and interviews].

Ronald Hayman, *Arnold Wesker.* Heinemann 1970 (Contemporary Playwrights Series). Updated edition with additional chapters, New York: Ungar, 1973. [Synoptic introduction.]

Glenda Leeming and Simon Trussler, *The Plays of Arnold Wesker.* London: Gollancz, 1971. [Detailed discussion of plays up to 1970.]

Glenda Leeming, *Arnold Wesker.* Longman, for the British Council, 1972 (Writers and their Work Series). [Short analytic introduction.]

Glenda Leeming, *Wesker the Playwright.* London: Methuen, 1983. [The only full-scale work on Wesker, with details on productions as well as texts.]

Articles and Chapters in Books

Richard Findlater, 'Plays and Politics, *Twentieth Century,* CLXVIII (1966), p.235-42.

John Dexter, 'Working with Arnold', *Plays and Players,* April 1962. [The director's view of their early collaboration.]

John Dexter, 'Chips and Devotion', *Plays and Players,* December 1962. [Description of the director's experience with rehearsals of *Chips with Everything.*]

Laurence Kitchin, 'Theatre in the Raw', *Mid-Century Drama.* London: Faber, 1962, p.98-114.

Laurence Kitchin, 'Drama with a Message: Arnold Wesker', in William A. Armstrong, ed., *Experimental Drama.* Bell, 1963, p.169-85. [Both the above give the feeling in the early 1960s of Wesker's significance.]

John Garforth, 'Arnold Wesker's Mission', in Charles Marowitz,

Tom Milne, and Owen Hale, eds., *The Encore Reader* (London: Methuen, 1965), p.223-30, reissued as *New Theatre Voices of the Fifties and Sixties* (London: Eyre Methuen, 1981).

John Russell Taylor, 'Productions out of Town', *Anger and After.* London: Methuen, revised edition, 1969, p.147-70. [Places Wesker in the context of the 'New Wave' dramatists of the late 1950s.]

Kingsley Amis, 'Not Talking about Jerusalem', in *What Became of Jane Austen?* (London, 1970), p.98-102.

Garry O'Connor, 'Wesker: a Voice Crying in the Wilderness', *Sunday Times Colour Supplement,* 10 May 1970, p.38-41. [Description of turbulent 'holiday' week spent by cast of *The Friends* together.]

Garry O'Connor, 'Production Casebook No. 2: Arnold Wesker's *The Friends', Theatre Quarterly,* I, 2 (1971), p.78-92. [Blow-by-blow account of Wesker's own explosive rehearsals for *The Friends.*]

John Russell Brown, 'Arnold Wesker: Theatrical Demonstration', *Theatre Language: a Study of Arden, Osborne, Pinter, and Wesker.* London: Allen Lane, 1972, p.158-89.

Michael Billington, 'When Did You Last See Your Arnold Wesker?', *The Guardian,* 13 May 1974. [Assessment of changing attitudes towards Wesker and his contemporaries.]

Margaret Drabble, 'Arnold Wesker', *New Review,* Feb. 1975, p.25-30.

Frank Coppieters, 'Arnold Wesker's Centre Fortytwo: a Cultural Revolution Betrayed', *Theatre Quarterly,* V, 18 (1975), p.37-51. [Full description of the development and decline of the Centre Fortytwo project.]

Catherine Itzin, 'Arnold Wesker', *Stages in the Revolution.* London: Eyre Methuen, 1980. [Traces the political strand in Wesker's development.]

Glenda Leeming, 'Articulacy and Awareness', in C.W.E. Bigsby, ed., *Contemporary English Dramatists* (Edward Arnold, 1981). [Relates the themes of the early plays to those of the 'seventies.]

Margery M. Morgan, 'Arnold Wesker: the Celebratory Instinct', in Hedwig Bock and Albert Wertheim, eds., *Essays on Contemporary British Drama* (Munich: Max Hueber Verlag).

Tapes

David Adland, *Roots.* Haslemere, Surrey: Studytapes, 1978. [Includes booklet.]

Christopher Bigsby, *Arnold Wesker.* British Council Literature Study Aids, 1977. [Includes booklet.]

David Wade, *The Dramatist Speaks: Arnold Wesker, 'Roots'.* London: Argo, 1979.